CW01346258

ELECTRONIC BANKING
The Legal Implications
Edited by R. M. Goode

The Institute of Bankers

Centre for Commercial Law Studies
Queen Mary College · University of London

First Published 1985

This book is copyright under the Berne Convention. All rights are reserved. Apart from any fair dealing for the purpose of private study, research, criticism or review, as permitted under the Copyright Act, 1956, no part of this publication may be reproduced, stored in a retrieval system, or transmitted in any form or by means, electronic, electrical, chemical, mechanical, optical, photocopying, recording or otherwise, without the prior permission of the copyright owner.

Enquiries should be sent to the publishers at the undermentioned address:

THE INSTITUTE OF BANKERS
10 Lombard Street
London EC3V 9AS

© The Institute of Bankers 1985 and Centre for Commercial Law Studies, Queen Mary College, University of London.

ISBN 0 85297 130 3

British Library Cataloguing in Publication Data

Electronic banking: the legal implications.
1. Banking law – Great Britain   2. Banks and banking – Great Britain – Data processing
I. Institute of Bankers
344.106'82   KD1715

ISBN 0 85297 130 3

Typeset in 10/11pt Times Roman
Text printed on 115 gsm Sequel Matt Cartridge, Cover on 132 gsm Fleet Chrome
by White Crescent Press Ltd, Luton, Beds, England

ELECTRONIC BANKING: THE LEGAL IMPLICATIONS

Page No

CONTENTS

Introduction – Roy Goode	v
Table of statutes	xiii
Table of cases	xv
Abbreviations and acronyms	xix
The contributors	xxi
1. Electronic Banking: An Overview of the Legal Implications – Eynon Smart	1
2. The Structure and Characteristics of the Principal Electronic Banking Systems – David Robinson	5
3. Electronic Funds Transfer as an Immediate Payment System – Roy Goode	15
4. Electronic Funds Transfer as a Deferred Settlement System – Peter Ellinger	29
5. Procedure and Evidence – Martin Karmel	45
6. Fraud, Error and System Malfunction: A Banker's Viewpoint – Jonathan Lass	57
7. Fraud, Error and System Malfunction: A Lawyer's Viewpoint – Robert Pennington	67
8. The Quantum and Limits of Liability – Eric Woods	83
9. The Electronic Presentation of Instruments – Anu Arora	105
10. The Electronic Presentation and Transfer of Shipping Documents – Alan Urbach	111
11. International Trade Data Interchange Systems – Bernard Wheble	123
Index	131

INTRODUCTION

Every autumn The Institute of Bankers and the Centre for Commercial Law Studies jointly organise a residential weekend seminar at which leading bankers and banking lawyers come together to discuss a specific area of banking law in the light of trends in domestic and international banking practice. The first seminar was devoted to The Legal Liability of Bankers; the second, to Changing Attitudes to Security, and the third, to another highly topical subject, Electronic Banking: The Legal Implications. This book reproduces, with tables and index, the papers presented at the third seminar, revised by the contributors and with an overview by Eynon Smart, reprinted by courtesy of the editor and publishers of *Banking World*. On behalf of the two organisations I should like to express our warm thanks to all the contributors.

David Robinson's paper outlines the main payment message systems currently used in England. As his description shows, payment messages are usually transmitted through one or more of three types of medium: paper, eg bills of exchange, cheques, bankers' payments, written direct debits and credit transfers; magnetic material, eg magnetic tapes, disks, cassettes; and purely electronic media, eg telephone, telex, electronic transmission between computers or between a terminal and a computer. Not infrequently such media will be employed in combination, as in the case of cheque truncation, where a cheque is issued and given to the payee's bank for collection but is retained by that bank, the data being transmitted electronically to the paying bank.

The characteristics of paper-based instructions and undertakings are that they embody a transaction in permanent form, are typically expressed in words and figures and are authenticated by a signature identifying the party giving the payment message. Paper-based messages cannot readily be altered without this fact appearing on the face of the document. Finally, delivery of the payment message usually takes a significant period of time – hours, days or even weeks.

Magnetic material shares with paper-based items the characteristic that the transfer medium is tangible and movable, so that messages stored on it cannot only be located but can be recalled prior to their delivery to the intended recipient. There, however, the resemblance ends. The payment message is expressed in computer code, the handwritten signature is replaced by an electronic key designed to authenticate the message and, in contrast to a paper message where the message itself is permanent and is retained on the original paper, the message on tape, disk, etc, may, in the absence of security measures, be altered, erased or transferred to other magnetic material without this fact being discoverable from an examination of the medium.

In the case of pure electronic funds transfer, the message is not carried in permanent form, though it is possible to have it logged during transmission. The time taken for delivery of the message depends on whether it is a purely bilateral transmission – as in the case of CHAPS, where a message sent by or through a participating bank is transmitted electronically direct to the recipient bank – or is routed through a clearing house or batching centre, as in BACS, where the messages have to be sorted and then batched by addressee before being sent forward, a process which even in a purely automated clearing system will take at least some hours. The delay resulting from the batching process is significant in at least two respects. First, it allows of an opportunity to recall a payment message which may be denied in a near-instantaneous system. Secondly, until the batching process is complete a clearing participant sending a payment message will not know its net position in relation to other participants.

My own paper examines the legal implications of EFT as an immediate payment system, concentrating on two particular questions: when does a payment message become irrevocable? and when is the transfer of funds to be considered complete? The latter question, which involves determination of the time of actual payment, does not seem to depend on the medium employed. The rules are the same for EFT as for paper-based systems. This is also largely true of the first question. The difference is that whereas the rules as to what constitutes payment can be formulated with a reasonable measure of assurance, the same is not true of the rules as to revocability of a payment instruction or undertaking, which remain obscure for most payment methods other than cheques and bills of exchange. In particular, it is unclear whether the message becomes binding on the sender when it is received or only when the recipient has acted upon it so as to change his position. Much useful work on this and related issues has been done by the United Nations Commission on International Trade Law. EFT may raise special considerations because of the possibility of technological breakdown or unauthorised interference with the message, but fundamentally the answer, if we knew it, should be the same for EFT as for paper-based credit transfers. It is in the interests of the efficiency of the payment mechanism as a whole to make messages irrevocable on receipt, as in the case of documentary credits, for if each party's commitment is to depend on his transferee's change of position the question whether the original message has become irrevocable will be capable of answer only by elaborate enquiry right down the chain.

Professor Ellinger discusses whether, and in what conditions, it is possible to simulate the term bill of exchange electronically. The first question is whether an EFT instruction given by a debtor to his own bank constitutes an assignment of funds. This receives a negative reply. Secondly, does it commit the debtor's bank to pay the creditor? Again, the answer is no. It is merely an authority to pay, addressed by the debtor to his bank and not by itself imposing on the bank any duty to the creditor. Each subsequent message generates a distinct agency relationship, but when funds are transferred from one agent bank to another it is not always easy to determine at what point the recipient bank ceases to be the agent of the transferor bank and becomes the agent of the creditor. If the transferee bank is instructed to hold the funds for a designated period before payment, can the transferor bank cancel the payment message during that period or is it irrevocable upon receipt? Different legal systems apparently provide different answers to this question.

Existing systems allow the storage of payment instructions, at least for some days, but to hold payment instructions in suspense for months would obviously raise technological problems of an entirely different order. Moreover, as Professor Ellinger points out, the bill of exchange is a negotiable instrument, and to reproduce electronically the characteristics of transferability by manual delivery and holder in due course status would be extremely difficult and expensive. Professor Ellinger concludes by questioning the need for replacement of the traditional bill or note by a deferred EFT system.

A major problem relating to computerised data is the acceptability of computer records as evidence of a payment instruction. If the party alleged to have sent the message, or to have withdrawn money from an ATM, disputes the fact, how is it to be established? Martin Karmel examines these questions in the light of current English legislation, and discusses the precautions that customers might be expected to take to prevent unauthorised operation of their account, a question long familiar to bankers in relation to cheques. Of great importance here is the onus of proof. Is there a presumption that the computer record is correct? That the system was functioning properly? That the message was given by the

ELECTRONIC BANKING – THE LEGAL IMPLICATIONS

customer concerned and not by an unauthorised third party? The need for answers to these questions will become more pressing with the introduction of electronic funds transfer at point of sale (EFTPOS).

This leads on naturally to the two papers on fraud, error and system malfunction. Jonathan Lass offers an overview of the problems of risk allocation as seen by a banker. Unauthorised interference with the payment system may take place at various stages and by various parties. Employees may have ready access both to written inputs into the computer system and to the system itself. Communications interference is a growing problem. One might add here that care needs to be taken concerning the fidelity of those who supply and maintain equipment. But fraud is not the only problem. As Mr Lass points out, system breakdown can have the most serious consequences for banks and their customers. The establishment of proper standards – a question to which the Banking Committee of the International Standards Organisation has been devoting much work – is of vital importance.

The lawyer's viewpoint on these issues is presented by Professor Robert Pennington in a detailed analysis of the case law on the rights and duties of banks and their customers in relation to unauthorised payment instructions. In what circumstances may a bank maintain a debit to its customer's account when paying without a mandate? What precautions is the customer expected to take to prevent fraud? For whose acts are the paying bank and the receiving bank legally responsible? Professor Pennington devotes particular attention to the operation of CHAPS when examining these questions, and concludes that the settlement bank's duty of care requires the installation and operation of reasonably effective security systems, which will need to be updated with additional defensive devices as new methods of perpetrating computer frauds emerge.

A characteristic feature of British domestic banking has been the remarkable informality of the arrangements between banker and customer. There is usually no written agreement at all, the contractual relationship being governed by oral discussion, brief letters and banking custom and practice. As Eric Woods points out, this is now beginning to change. In the case of credit cards there is invariably a detailed printed agreement setting out the terms of issue of the card and the responsibilities of the cardholder. The introduction of EFT, and the possibility of large-scale fraud, may well lead to a more general use of agreements, with clauses limiting the banker's liability. Mr Woods discusses the utility of such clauses in the light of developing case law on inequality of bargaining power and the Unfair Contract Terms Act 1977 and in the context of six examples of breakdown in the payment mechanism. He then goes on to emphasise the need for care in drafting the contract terms and instructions to staff, moves on to discuss the United States legislation on EFT and then the crucial question how far a bank may reasonably restrict by contract either its liability or the service it is prepared to offer.

And this raises the whole question how far the evolution of banking technology helps the domestic customer. The huge growth in the volume of cheques and other payment instructions clearly necessitated replacement of manual operations with computerised systems. That these have proved of great benefit to bankers and their customers cannot be questioned. The customer can withdraw cash from an ATM, check the state of his account when he likes, initiate payment instructions from his own home and enjoy a range of other benefits conferred by computerisation. But not all advances have been progress. The customer is expected to take precautions against improper use of his account, yet is denied easy facilities for doing so. No longer are his cheques returned to him. No longer does his bank statement identify each payee. Instead, he has to retain all his cheque stubs and match them laboriously against his bank statement. Banks who seek in the future to restrict their liability for the consequences of fraud would do well to consider whether it might not be to their advantage, as well as that of their customers, to give more information on bank statements, so that the customer is able to tell at a glance whether something is amiss.

Cheque truncation, the subject of Dr Arora's paper, is a halfway house between normal cheque clearance and electronic funds transfer. The cheque is given to the payee's bank for collection but instead of being physically presented to the paying bank it is retained by the collecting bank, eg at its clearing office or another central location, and relevant data are transmitted electronically to the paying bank. As Dr Arora's paper shows, cheque truncation, still being developed in this country, is already in use in Europe and the United States. The 1984 Australian draft Cheques Bill also made provision for cheque truncation, the paying bank being entitled to call for the original cheque if it wished. One of the major problems, in theory at any rate, is that the signature on the original cheque is seen not by the drawer's bank but by that of the payee, which has no way of knowing (unless the drawer is also its customer) whether the signature is genuine or not. I say 'in theory' because in modern banking practice verification of the signature is fast disappearing in any event, since the volume of cheques in issue is far too great to allow for individual scrutiny of the kind which signature requirement envisages. If, however, the handwritten signature were to disappear and be replaced by an electronic authenticating key known only to the drawer and his bank, this would open the way to electronic verification of the 'signature' and thereby overcome this particular problem.

Electronic funds transfer is already with us in limited form. Much harder to achieve is its trade counterpart, the electronic transmission of trade data, designed to avoid the expense and delay involved in successive movements of large numbers of shipping documents. Alan Urbach explains why delay occurs and the various solutions propounded to deal with the problem. In theory, at least, there is no reason why trade data cannot be transmitted electronically in the same way as financial data. In practice, it is much more complex, partly because the volume of data is much greater and partly because the shipping industry is a great deal more diffuse than the banking community, so that the general adoption of compatible equipment presents huge problems.

An ingenious halfway house, in the construction of which Mr Urbach has been heavily engaged for some years, is the Intertanko/Chase Manhattan project for a central registry, known as SeaDocs, for the deposit of bills of lading. The bill of lading would be issued to the shipper in the conventional manner and would then be deposited by him in the SeaDocs Registry, which would hold it to his order. If the shipper wished to transfer the goods, he would instruct the Registry to indorse the bill in favour of the transferee. The bill would remain in the possession of the Registry, but as agent of the transferee. A similar process would be adopted for subsequent transfers. It would, of course, be necessary to establish a sound security system for authentication and confirmation of transfer instructions. The concept is ingenious, and if implemented could help to overcome problems of delay which are caused by the need to move the bill of lading physically through a number of hands, including those of issuing and advising banks involved in a documentary credit.

However, in the final paper in this book Bernard Wheble draws attention to a number of legal problems that will have to be surmounted if the traditional bill of lading is to be displaced by an automated data processing (ADP). These problems – writing, sig-

INTRODUCTION

nature and evidence – mirror those previously raised in relation to electronic funds transfer. Much useful work on ADP has already been done by the UN Economic Commission for Europe, and many of the legal issues discussed are equally applicable to EFT.

The present volume does not pretend to offer solutions to these numerous complex problems. What it seeks to do is to identify the issues, to demonstrate the potential impact of existing laws on the development of EFT and to point the way to more intensive studies in the future. It will, I hope, prove of interest not only to bankers and lawyers but to all those who are involved in the mechanism of payment.

The production of this book owes much to the labours of Alan Miller, Under-Secretary of The Institute of Bankers, to Eynon Smart, a well-known writer on banking law, and to Tony Drury, who provided editorial assistance in the early stages. We are also indebted to Mrs Anne Lyons for the excellent index, and to Miss Hilary Norman who so ably undertook the design work.

R. M. Goode

Centre for Commercial Law Studies,
Queen Mary College,
13th August 1985

TABLE OF STATUTES

Bankers' Books Evidence Act 1879 . . . . 2, 45
    s. 10 46
Banking Act 1979
    6th Schedule 46
Bills of Exchange Act 1882 . . . . 2, 126
    s. 2 . . . . 39, 41
       3(1) 34, 39
       8 34
       4 43
       17 40
       21 . . . . 34, 42
       29 41
       31 . . . . 41, 42
       32(2)(3) 34
       38 41
       40(2) 43
       43(2) 41
       45(1) 43
       47(2) 41
       48, 49 43
       51 43
       52(3) 43
       54 . . . . 40, 42
       55(1) 30, 41
       55(2) 41
       69, 70 42
       75(1) 30
       79(2) 42
Civil Evidence Act 1968 . . . . 2, 46, 48
    s. 5 . . . . 46, 48, 53–4, 56, 132
Consumer Credit Act 1974
    s. 83 . . . . 52, 96
       84 52
       84(1) 61
County of Kent Act 1981
    s. 82 47
Criminal Evidence Act 1965 . . . . 2, 46–9
    s. 1 56
       1(1) 48, 49

Electronic Funds Transfer Act 1978 (Title IX of the
Consumer Protection Act) (USA) 63, 64, 95
   s. 903 (6) 45
   908 .... 51, 95–6, 98–9
   909 .... 51, 61, 95–6, 100–1
Law of Property Act 1925
   s. 136 35
Limitation Act 1980
   s. 5, 32(1) 81
Misrepresentation Act 1967
   s. 3 102
Misrepresentation Act (Northern Ireland) 1967
   s. 3 102
Police and Criminal Evidence Act 1984
   Part VII; s. 69 .... 47, 48
Powers of Attorney Act 1971
   s. 4 (1) 38
Supply of Goods and Services Act 1982 .... 58, 63
   s. 13 75
Unfair Contract Terms Act 1977 .... ix, 2, 58, 61, 85, 87, 89, 90
   s. 2 .... 101, 103
      2 (2) 36
      3 .... 82, 88, 90, 102
      11 .... 36, 88, 102
      13 .... 96, 103
      schedule 2 .... 101, 103

Rules of the Supreme Court

Order 38
   rule 21 56
       24 .... 48, 54–6

TABLE OF CASES

Aiken v Short (1856) 1 H & N 210 69
Alan (W. J.) & Co Ltd v El Nasr Export & Import Co [1972] 2 All ER 127 17
Auchteroni v Midland Bank Ltd [1928] 2 KB 294 74
Babcock v Lawson (1879) 4 QBD 394 69
Barclays Bank Ltd v W J Sims Son and Cooke (Southern) Ltd [1980] QB 677 .... 80, 81
Barker v Wilson [1980] 1 WLR 884 46
Barwick v English Joint Stock Bank (1867) LR 2 Ex 259 77
Bayly, Martin & Fay Inc v Kenny, unreported, 80 Civ 82 CSH of 18 February 1982 35
Bellamy v Majoribanks (1852) 7 Exch 389 73
Bird & Co v Thomas Cook & Son Ltd [1937] 2 All ER 227 39
Birmingham Banking Co (1868) LR 3 Ch App 651 39
Brimnes, The [1975] QB 929 36
Brinkibon Ltd v Stahag Stahl and Stahlwarenhandlesgesellschaft mbH [1983] 2 A.C. 34 25
Brook v Hook (1871) LR 6 Ex 89 71
Broom v Hall (1859) 7 CBNS 503 68
Brown v Westminster Bank Ltd [1964] 2 Lloyd's Rep 187 71
Calico Printers' Association v Barclays Bank Ltd (1930) 36 Com Cas 71 .... 36, 73
Castle v Cross [1984] 1 WLR 1372 .... 49, 50
Catlin v Cyprus Finance Corpn (London) Ltd [1983] QB 759 70
Chambers v Miller (1862) 13 CBNS 125 .... 70, 80
Chase Manhattan Bank v Equibank, 394 F Supp 352, (1975) 39
Chatterton v London County Bank Ltd (1890) *The Miller*, 3rd November, 394 62
Chikuma, The [1981] 1 WLR 314 .... 36, 37
Clark v Oriental Bank Corporation (1878) 3 App Cas 325 73
Cocks v Masterman (1829) 9 B & C 280 .... 79, 81
Cundy v Lindsay (1878) 3 App Cas 459 69
Delbrueck v Manufacturers' Hanover Trust Co, 609 F 2d 1047, (1979) 35, 36
Deutsche Bank v Beriro & Co (1895) 73 LT 669 70
Equitable Trust Company of New York v Dawson Partners Ltd (1927) 27 L1LR 49 .... 36, 77
Esso Petroleum Limited v Harper's Garage (Stourport) Limited [1967] 1 All ER 699 85
Evra Corporation v Swiss Bank Corporation 673F 2d 951 (1982) 35, 36, 63

xv

TABLE OF CASES

Farrows Bank Ltd, Re [1923] 1 Ch 41 18
Foley v Hill (1848) 2 HLC 28 73
Griffin v Weatherby (1868) L.R.3 Q.B753 19
Guaranty Trust Co of New York v Lyon, 124 NYS 2d 680 (1953) 36
Hadley v Baxendale (1854) 9 Ex 341 63
Hardman v Booth (1853) 1 H & C 803 69
Hare v Henty (1861) 10 CBNS 66 68
Imperial Bank of Canada v Bank of Hamilton [1903] AC 49 79
Junior Books Ltd v The Veitchi Co Ltd [1982] 3 WLR 477 63
Karak Rubber Co Ltd v Burden (No 2) [1972] 1 All ER 1210 ... 75
Kepitagalla Rubber Estate Ltd v National Bank of India [1909] 2 KB 1010 72
Liggett (Liverpool) Ltd v Barclays Bank Ltd [1928] 1 KB 46 ... 71, 74
Lloyd v Grace, Smith & Co [1912] AC 716 77
Lloyds Bank Ltd v Bundy [1975] QB 326 86
London and River Plate Bank Ltd v Bank of Liverpool Ltd [1896] 1 QB 7 79
London Intercontinental Trust Ltd v Barclays Bank Ltd [1980] 1 Lloyd's Rep 241 71
London Joint Stock Bank v Macmillan & Arthur [1918] AC 777 .... 30, 61, 72
M'Kenzie v British Linen Co (1881) 6 App Cas 82, 99 71
Mackersy v Ramsays Bonar and Co (1843) 9 Cl & F 818 73
Mahony v East Holyford Mining Co (1875) LR 7 HL 869 70
E. D. & F. Man v Nigerian Sweets & Confectionery Co Ltd [1972] 2 Lloyd's Rep 50 17
Mardorf Peach & Co Ltd v Attica Sea Carriers Corpn of Liberia [1977] AC 850 .... 26, 36, 78
Momm v Barclays Bank International [1977] QB 790 .. 22, 26, 36, 91
Moorcock, The (1889) 14 PD 64 88
Morrell v Wootton (1852) 16 Beav 197 78
Morris v Bethall (1869) LR 5 CP 47 71
Myers v DPP [1965] AC 1001 46
National Westminster Bank v Barclays Bank International Ltd [1975] QB 654 .... 79, 80, 81
Ognibene v Citibank NA 446 NYS 2d 845 (1981) 61
Orr v Union Bank (1854) 1 Macq HL 315 .... 70, 74
Pettman v Keble (1805) 9 CB 701 68
Photo Production Ltd v Securicor [1980] 1 All ER 556 87
Pollard v Bank of England (1871) LR 6QB 623 70
R v Ewing [1983] QB 1039; [1983] 2 All ER 645, CA 56
R v Kohn [1979] Crim LR 675 42

xvi

TABLE OF CASES

R v Pettigrew (1980) 71 Cr App R 39 .... 49, 50
R v Wood (1983) 76 Cr App Rep 23 .... 48, 49, 50
Reigate v Union Manufacturing Co [1918] 1 KB 592 89
Rekstin v Severo Sibirsko Gosudarstvennoe Akcionerno [1933] 1 KB 33 .... 35, 36
Robarts v Tucker (1851) 16 QB 560 74
Royal Products Ltd v Midland Bank Ltd [1981] 2 Lloyd's Rep 194 .... 18, 35, 36
A Schroeder Music Publishing Co Ltd v Macaulay [1974] 3 All ER 616 86
Selangor United Rubber Estates Ltd v Cradock (No 3) [1968] 2 All ER 1073 75
Singer v Yokohama Specie Bank, 47 NYS 2d 881 (1944) 36
Smart v Sandars (1848) 5 CB 895 38
Tai Hing Cotton Mill Ltd v Liu Chong Hing Bank Ltd [1985] 2 All ER 947 72
Tournier v National Provincial and Union Bank of England [1924] 1 KB 461 64
Walker v Rostron (1842) 9 M & W 41 19
Warlow v Harrison (1859) 1 E & E 709 19
Westminster Bank Ltd v Hilton (1926) 43 TLR 124 ...... 30, 68
White v Gordon (1851) 10 CB 919 69
Wilkinson v Johnson (1824) 3 B & C 428 .... 79, 81
Williams v Atlantic Assurance Co [1933] 1 KB 1 35

ABBREVIATIONS AND ACRONYMS

ACH	Automated Clearing House.
ACL	Atlantic Container Lines.
ADP	Automated Data Processing.
ATM	Automated Teller Machine.
BACS	Bankers' Automated Clearing Services.
BBEA	Bankers' Books Evidence Act 1879.
BEA	Bills of Exchange Act 1882.
B/L	Bill of Lading.
CARDIS	Cargo Data Interchange Systems.
CD	Cash Dispenser.
CEDEL	Centale de Livraison de Valeurs Mobilières.
CHAPS	Clearing House Automated Payment System.
CHIPS	Clearing House Interbank Payments System.
CIF	Cost, Insurance, Freight.
EDP	Electronic Data Processing.
EFT	Electronic Funds Transfer.
EFTPOS	Electronic Funds Transfer at the Point of Sale.
EUROCLEAR	European Clearing System for Euro-banks.
GPO	General Post Office.
IBRO	Inter-Bank Research Organisation.
ISO	International Standards Organisation.
LOI	Letter of Indemnity.
NCITD	(US) National Committee of International Trade Procedures.
PIN	Personal Identification Number.
PSS	Packet Switching Service.
SeaDocs	Seaborne Trade Documentation System.
SID	Swift Interface Device.
SITPRO	Simplification of Trade Procedure Board.
SWIFT	Society for Worldwide Interbank Financial Telecommunications.
TALISMAN	Transfer Accounting Lodgement for Investors, Stock Management for Jobbers
TDIS	Trade Data Interchange Systems.
t/t	Telegraphic transfer.
UCP	Uniform Customs and Practice for Documentary Credits.
UCTA	Unfair Contract Terms Act 1977.

CONTRIBUTORS

Professor Roy Goode, OBE, LLD – Crowther Professor of Credit and Commercial Law, Director of the Centre for Commercial Law Studies, Queen Mary College, University of London.

Eynon Smart, Hon FIB, LLB – The Institute of Bankers.

David Robinson, BSc – General Manager, Consumer Banking Services, The Royal Bank of Scotland, Inter-Bank Committee on Electronic Funds Transfer at the Point of Sale.

Professor Peter Ellinger, MJur, DPhil – Sir John Barry Professor of Law, Monash University.

Martin Karmel, MA, BCL – Senior Deputy Secretary, The Committee of London and Scottish Bankers and the British Bankers' Association.

Jonathan D. Lass, MA, Solicitor, Vice President and Senior Regional Counsel, Citibank NA, London.

Professor Robert R. Pennington, LLD, Professor of Commercial Law, Birmingham University.

Eric Woods, LLM, Principal Solicitor, Midland Bank.

Dr Anu Arora, Lecturer in Law, University of Liverpool, formerly Lecturer in Law, Queen Mary College.

Alan Urbach, MBA, MA, Inventor of the SeaDocs system set up by the Chase Manhattan Bank for automating the handling of seabourne trade documentation; Executive Director of Trade Finance, Elders Finance and Investment Co. Ltd., Melbourne; former Vice-President and Project Director, Chase Manhattan Bank.

Bernard Wheble, CBE, Hon FIB – Hon Chairman, International Chamber of Commerce Commission on Banking Technique and Practice.

ELECTRONIC BANKING
An Overview of the Legal Implications*

Eynon Smart

The optimist may suggest that there is nothing fundamentally new in electronic funds transfer; it is merely a variety of novel methods of transferring funds from D to C, and in banking any legal problems will be solved by analogy with existing law. The relationship of banker and customer is fairly well settled, and all that will be needed is the fitting of changed methods into an established framework. But optimism, based on a partial truth, oversimplifies the matter. Certainly the cheque, which commits the paying banker only when he decides to pay it (and which gives the unpaid payee a right of action against the drawer), is an uncertain basis for analogy.

Telex, and long before it the telephone, familiarised bankers with paperless transfers; and EFT itself, most popularly in the shape of ATMs, has been in use for some years. But we have seen so far only the first steps on a path that can already lead to computer-to-computer transfers, with home banking and EFTPOS on the way. And when we see in CHAPS a transfer originating from the customer of a non-settlement bank passing to a customer of another non-settlement bank we have an inter-relationship of creditor and debtor with perhaps four banks intervening, producing interesting questions as to the rights and liabilities of the parties.

Even with paper-based transfers, by direct debit or credit transfer, there are unresolved uncertainties – in particular, at what stage in the normal clearing process does a payment become irrevocable? The clearing rules do not always provide an answer, and where a clearing rule is lacking there is no helpful analogy for EFT. Banking practice in the new technology is hardly yet sufficiently established to provide the guidance that the courts would look for; and the potential complications of effectively coping with the period of bankers' blind exposure, in, for example, the BACS batching process, are alarming. Clear and published rules might avoid some of the litigation that almost certainly lies ahead.

This is to consider only immediate payment transfers between debtor and creditor, with whatever intermediaries a particular system makes necessary. Deferred payments by EFT are possible, for instance through BACS, but it seems unlikely that bankers will develop a system which, *inter alia*, would make it difficult for them to accept their customers' countermand instructions. And while it is possible to produce by EFT a kind of equivalent of the bill of exchange (the bill of lading is already being processed electronically, for example by SeaDocs in a central registry) the bill of exchange has peculiar properties that make it an unlikely candidate for electronic handling. It represents a succession of contracts; with every party acquiring rights and liabilities; it is a document requiring presentation, and it is itself an item of property. The difficulties of translating all this in electronic terms make any such translation unlikely in the foreseeable future.

The various rights and liabilities involved in EFT can of course be covered in whatever *ad hoc* contracts are used for particular techniques. British banks have always stopped short of devising a basic contract covering the general banker/customer relationship, on the lines of the useful practice in many other countries, but this has not deterred them from producing innumerable contracts for specific transactions in conventional banking, and in EFT similar specific contracts have appeared. In a kind of parallel evolution, Britain has a minimum of legislation relevant to EFT, in contrast to, say, America and Australia, where legislative provisions may provide pointers to the development of British practice.

In the legislative field, with the background thought that the Bills of Exchange Act may eventually need amendment to accommodate electronic activity, bankers have the acceptance by the courts, now confirmed in legislation, of electronic evidence by way of an extension of the Bankers' Books Evidence Act; and they have to consider the possible relevance of the Unfair Contract Terms Act to their new specific contracts, and the varying requirements of evidence submitted under the Civil Evidence Act and the Criminal Evidence Act. Evidence – and proof – have their own problems in EFT. What does a bank do when a customer is prepared to aver on oath that his credit card has never left his possession and that his PIN has never been disclosed even to his wife?

Fraud, error and technical malfunction in EFT pose in some peculiar ways the basic question that has been asked in banking for centuries: where does the liability lie? – when the computer breaks down, when the electricity supply fails, when (improbably) a GPO landline is tapped. The banker's 'due care' seems likely to be expanded as the technology develops: his electronic systems will need regular updating to match rapidly changing times.

The introduction of truncation in the cheque clearing process has produced its own EFT-related problem. When the paying banker can be given electronically all the information he needs to debit his customer's account, is it essential for the cheque itself to be transported to him? The economies in time and labour of full truncation would clearly be substantial, but although partial truncation (of cheques drawn on one branch of a bank by customers of other branches of the same bank) is being tried, the banks are thinking hard before going further. The cheque, like the bill of exchange, can be more than a bare order to pay. How long is the collecting banker to store the cheques he retains? The paying banker has to see the backs as well as the fronts of the cheques he pays, both to see the endorsements on the diminishing number of 'R' cheques and to see the cheque card number written on the back of the increasing number of cheques guaranteed by cheque cards. And whether or not drawers' signatures are as carefully scrutinised as they used to be, they are still the authentication of the customer's mandate.

That mandate is of course fundamental in the banker/customer relationship, and within the wide range of paperless transfers it poses a number of questions. Can a signature be effectively verified in an electronic transmission, and will such transmission make it harder to see alterations?

How effective legally is the replacement of the customer's signature by his PIN? How much does the customer know of the method of transmission the banker proposes to use? And, as a very substantial expansion of a risk as old as the telephone, what of the corporate treasurer authorising a number of his officials to give telephone instructions for very large transfers of funds?

The legal problem of paperless transmission intermingled with the practical difficulties, have a different dimension when the full benefits of international usage are sought. SWIFT is an established and growing concern, with its own peculiarities. Compatibility of hardware is a practical problem, but it can have its legal implications in some of the areas here touched upon. The requirements of data protection, considerable within a single country, are magnified in the complications of cross-border activity.

Technologists tend to argue that when a technology is possible it should be used. Bankers, at home and abroad, confronted by massive volume growth and unprecedented competition, have moved into unfamiliar techniques much more promptly than might have been expected in a traditionally cautious calling. They have had to balance profit (and perhaps survival) against uncovered risks and they may be uncomfortably exposed in some areas of electronic development. But we may believe that the risks are identified: bankers are not waiting for them to take shape in litigation.

* This review of the topics discussed at the third annual seminar on Banking Law held by The Institute of Bankers and the Centre for Commercial Law Studies, Queen Mary College, in November 1984 is reproduced from *Banking World*, February 1985, by kind permission of the Editor and Publisher.

THE STRUCTURE AND CHARACTERISTICS OF THE PRINCIPAL ELECTRONIC BANKING SYSTEMS

David Robinson

The purpose of this paper is to give a general picture of the main electronic banking systems as a basis for the detailed discussions which are expected to take place during the rest of the Seminar. The trend in the various systems is clear, namely, from the paper-based systems which have been in operation for many years through the automated off-line system of BACS to the more recent on-line CHAPS and, still to be introduced, EFTPOS. The paper follows this trend and is split into three sections. It leans heavily on background work done by the Inter-Bank Research Organisation for the Child Committee who in 1984, on behalf of the member banks of the Bankers' Clearing House, reviewed the organisation, membership and control of payment clearing systems.

Paper-based systems

General Clearing (debit)
This is based on the collecting bank branch (ie the branch at which the cheque has been paid in) presenting the cheque for payment to the drawee or paying bank branch (ie the branch which holds the account on which the cheque is drawn) via the banks' respective clearing departments. Each bank branch sends cheques for collection to its clearing centre in London, where cheques for the other banks are amalgamated. These are then exchanged with the other banks, who agree the amounts concerned, sort the cheques into branch order and pass them to the branches on which they are drawn. Settlement takes place on a net basis, the figures being agreed prior to daily settlement at the Bank of England. The time-cycle for the General Clearing is essentially three business days. Cheques paid in at a bank branch on day one are exchanged on day two with settlement taking place, and customers' accounts being updated, on day three.

Consideration is being given at present to the possible introduction of a system of cheque truncation where the information on certain cheques will be presented, rather than the cheque itself.

Credit Clearing

This operates in a similar way to the General Clearing for cheques and is part of the Bank Giro system – the name given to the credit transfer system by which credit vouchers may be transferred between banks. Branches send the credit vouchers to their clearing departments where they are amalgamated for delivery to the other banks at the Clearing House. The automation of the system is well advanced, thereby enabling credit vouchers to be processed in a manner similar to cheques.

Town Clearing

Town Clearing is the system for same-day settlement of large value cheques (£10,000 and over) drawn on and paid into clearing bank branches within the designated Town Clearing area of the City. The system operates on a strict time-table. Each of the banks sorts eligible cheques drawn on the other member banks into bundles known as charges. These charges are then delivered to the respective representatives of the other banks at the Clearing House. The total of the cheques in a charge will then be agreed by the receiving bank and the cheques sorted into branch order and taken to the branches on which they are drawn for scrutiny before payment is made. Unpaid cheques must be returned that day to the presenting bank through the Clearing House. At the end of the clearing each bank agrees with each receiving bank the total of cheques presented.

Settlement

Settlement is effected each business day across accounts at the Bank of England for the balances of that day's Town Clearing, work exchanged in the previous day's Debit and Credit Clearings and work processed by BACS also on the previous day. Each bank completes a daily settlement sheet which shows for Town Clearing the balances due to be paid to, and received from, the other banks and the bank's net charge or pay figure for the other clearings. The figures for the previous day's clearings can be entered in the morning but the final net balances cannot be calculated until after the end of Town Clearing, normally between 4.30 pm and 4.45 pm. Each bank then completes a ticket showing its net position and these are taken to the Inspector who checks the figures against the settlement sheets and signs the tickets. These are then divided in two. One half is given to the Bank of England representative and forms the instruction on which the Bank adjusts the bank's accounts with it. The other half is returned to the bank as a record.

Other clearing channels

Inter-branch
Not all paper cheques and credits pass through the Clearing House. Some 37 per cent of all such items in 1983 were drawn on or credited to the same bank into which they were paid and were dealt with through the inter-branch system.

These items are sent by the individual branches to the banks' head offices or clearing departments where they are listed, sorted into branch order and re-listed before despatch on the same day.

Walks
Prior to the introduction of agency arrangements in 1974 non-clearing bank cheques presented at clearing bank branches were sent to the banks' clearing departments and then 'walked' round to the London office of the non-clearing institution for presentation for payment. Where the non-clearing bank office was outside London, they were posted to that office or to the nearest branch of the clearing bank who then walked the cheques round to the non-clearer's office. This system was continued for some institutions or bodies (mainly government departments in recent years) but the volume was reduced substantially by the introduction of agency arrangements. Efforts have been made to persuade institutions which have relied on the 'walks' system to appoint an agent so that their paper can be processed through a clearing bank and collected through the General Clearing. These have been generally successful.

Scottish and Irish cheques
Cheques drawn on branches of banks in Scotland are cleared by sending them direct, or via London offices, to their head offices in Edinburgh or Glasgow.

Items drawn on branches of banks in Ireland are sent direct to an Irish Bank which acts as an agent for the London clearing bank.

Clearing statistics (1983)

	Volumes (mn items)	*Value* (£bn)
General debit:		
inter-bank	1,672	543
inter-branch	552	N/A

Clearing statistics (1983) *(continued)*

	Volumes (mn items)	Value (£bn)
Town:		
inter-bank	5	6,258
inter-branch	1	1,337
Credit:		
inter-bank	178	68
inter-branch	250	264
Total	2,658	N/A

Off-line electronic systems

Bankers' Automated Clearing Services (BACS) history
Bankers' Automated Clearing Services Limited was registered as a private limited liability company in September 1971 and began trading in December 1971. Prior to that – and since 1968 – the electronic transfer of funds between banks had been undertaken under the aegis of the Inter-Bank Computer Bureau.

Function
The function of BACS is to provide a cost effective Automated Clearing House service for inter-bank clearing of payment and collection transactions originated by either the sponsoring banks, or such other banks and corporate customers whom the sponsoring banks may sponsor to use the service.

BACS accepts files of transactions to be cleared on magnetic media of various kinds as well as by telecommunication links. Input is either direct from corporate customers (for credits and direct debits) or from banks (for standing orders and claims for unpaid cheques). The transactions are sorted to receiving banks and the information presented to the banks on magnetic tape.

BACS now processes 21 per cent of all sterling inter-bank clearings and the aim of the BACS Board is to increase this to 40 per cent by the end of the decade.

The operating time cycle covers three days, input being handed to BACS two days before the items are due to be credited to, or debited from, accounts. The input day deadline to BACS is 9.00 pm for customer input and 12.00 midnight (10.30 pm before June 1984) for certain categories of bank input, with output to the banks being available from about 3.00 am on day two.

Having effected the inter-bank clearing, BACS advises the Bankers' Clearing House and the sponsoring banks of the settlements which need to be made between them to conclude the clearing operation. There is no float created by the system, all file contra entries being applied on the same day as the file to which the contra relates.

BACS: volumes (1983)

	mn items		per cent	
Bank input	206		33	
of which: Standing orders		192		31
Claims for unpaid cheques		14		2
Customer input	408		67	
of which: Direct Debits		241		40
Credits		167		27
	614		100	

Values in 1983 were as follows:
  Credits and standing orders £105.3 bn
  Direct debits   £49.3 bn

On-line electronic systems

Clearing House Automated Payment System (CHAPS)
function
CHAPS is a developing system, additional to existing payments services, which came into operation on 9 February 1984. It is an electronic sterling credit transfer service developed by the current twelve settlement banks. Unlike BACS, CHAPS is not a central clearing system but involves bilateral transfer instructions from one bank to another. CHAPS offers the following features:

Same-day settlement: a nationwide alternative to the Town Clearing or telephonic transfers for payments of value £10,000 and above.

Wide access: individual settlement banks may offer use of the system to their customers, including non-settlement banks and other financial institutions. Instructions to issue a CHAPS payment message can be made in writing, by telex, by terminal or main-frame computer link-ups, or through a SWIFT terminal.

Guaranteed payments: each payment must be honoured by the settlement bank sending it, whether the payment is made by the settlement bank on its own behalf or on behalf of a customer. Payments must consequently be 'clean' eg, not conditional upon delivery of a document or evidence of title.

Hours of operation: all settlement banks must be able to receive payments from 9.30 am each business day and to 'cut off' the service at 3.00 pm, and thereafter to settle as soon as possible with each other, across their accounts at the Bank of England.

Each settlement bank has, or shares, two Tandem computers, of which one is for standby purposes; these are referred to as CHAPS gateways. Payment messages are transmitted between gateways across British Telecom's Packet Switchedstream Service. The gateways handle connection, recovery, message passing, acknowledgment, reconciliation, cut-off and settlement. Security features include encryption and end-to-end authentication.

Chaps volumes and values (November 1983)

Average number of payments per day	Average daily total value (£ million)	Average value per payment (£000s)
6,476	4,490	693

In the early days of the system, transaction values of between £10,000 and £100,000 were imposed by the Policy Committee. The upper limit was progressively raised and then removed from 1 May 1984. There are no plans at present to reduce the lower limit although this possibility is kept under review. It has been estimated that up to 30,000 sterling transactions of £10,000 or over are made each day.

Electronic funds transfer at point of sale (EFTPOS)

Function and system description
The proposed EFTPOS is a payment system which will allow

THE STRUCTURE AND CHARACTERISTICS OF THE PRINCIPAL ELECTRONIC BANKING SYSTEMS

retail payments to be made by transferring funds electronically from accounts of customers to the accounts of retailers for the settlement of purchases. Payments will thus be made without the need for cash, cheques or paper vouchers.

The essential elements of such a system are:
- electronic terminal equipment installed in retail premises;
- magnetically-striped plastic cards which may be either debit or credit cards and associated personal identification numbers (PINs), issued to customers by banks and other organisations;
- an automated message transmission system which links the terminal equipment with computers of the banks, credit card companies and other organisations holding the retailers' and customers' accounts (for ease of explanation the term 'bank' is used hereafter). Under present thinking, British Telecom's Packet Switching Service (PSS) will probably be used as it is the only practical network currently available.

It is intended that EFTPOS will be an additional payment system and customers will retain their choice of alternative media.

An EFTPOS transaction can be broken down into the following steps:
- when a customer wishes to pay by EFTPOS, his card will be passed through the reader in the terminal and the amount of the payment entered;
- vital information will be encrypted and sent with other details over the data communication network to the card issuer; a 'duplicate' (audit copy) will be sent to the retailer's 'bank';
- if the card-holder's account is in order the retailer will be informed that the transaction will be accepted provided the customer has the correct PIN;
- the customer will then enter the PIN on a special keyboard designed to shield the operation from onlookers. The PIN will be protected at all times to ensure complete security;
- provided the correct PIN has been entered, the terminal accepts the transaction and prints a confirmation;
- a message is transmitted to the card issuer confirming acceptance; a 'duplicate' (audit copy) will be sent to the retailer's 'bank';
- the amount of the purchase will be debited from the card-holder's account and credited to the retailer's account. The card-holder and the retailer will know from the outset when these entries will be passed. However, a refund facility will be provided.

c

It is likely that an EFTPOS transaction will be irrevocable after acceptance. Such a system could be operational twenty-four hours a day, seven days a week, and could be accessible to retailers and other parties anywhere in Great Britain. The system will be an on-line operation and all cards conforming with the standard will be technically acceptable. The system should always be 'in balance' in that settlement should occur among the 'banks' and card issuers for each day's work when totals have been agreed. The debiting and crediting cycles of card-holders and retailers should be determined independently by card issuers and banks.

Society for Worldwide Interbank Financial Telecommunications (SWIFT)

History
SWIFT was founded in 1973 by 239 European, American and Canadian banks in the form of a non-profit making society under Belgian law, with headquarters in Brussels. It became operational in May 1977 and within a few months all the initial 15 countries, including the United Kingdom, were connected. In March 1984 SWIFT had 1,122 member banks, passing about 0.4mn transactions per day through the system. By October 1983 the number of countries* had risen to 53, of which 37 were in live operation. Agreements were reached with CEDEL in 1981 and Mastercard and Euro-clear in 1982.

Function
The primary objective is to provide a network for members to convey rapid instructions to transfer money between themselves. Among the requirements are:
– constant availability; although individual members are committed only to being connected for seven hours per day during normal working hours in their time zone;
– security: SWIFT takes responsibility for this between points of connection with member's circuits, using packet-switching techniques over dedicated lines passing through linked operating centres in Belgium, the Netherlands and the United States. The UK uses the Dutch centre via SWIFT's regional processor at the BACS premises in Edgware, Middlesex;

*Or constitutional entities. For example Channel Islands and Isle of Man are counted separately from the UK.

- standardisation: of form of message, with prompts and instructions to operators in their own language;
- auditability: of all activity in the system by members;
- controllability: with several levels of input, audit and verification within the sending member's premises.

Member banks interface to SWIFT through either a SWIFT Interface Device (SID) supplied by Burroughs, General Automation or ICL, but with software provided by SWIFT, or by competitors' products meeting SWIFT's technical requirements. SWIFT's subsidiary company, SWIFT Terminal Services, based in Brussels, markets interface systems known as ST200 and ST500. Banks are responsible for messages between themselves and their regional processor.

The following categories of message are in use: customer transfers, bank transfers, currency operations, collections, documentary credits and securities. In addition SWIFT provides settlement services for CEDEL in the International Bond market.

ELECTRONIC FUNDS TRANSFER AS AN IMMEDIATE PAYMENT SYSTEM

Roy Goode

'Plus ça change, plus c'est la même chose.' No doubt prompted by this aphorism, one delegate at the International Bar Association's conference in Vienna earlier this year felt driven to ask, during a seminar on electronic funds transfer held by the Banking Law Committee, whether EFT was conceptually different from the physical carriage of money from one bank to another. In short, was there anything to talk about? The question deserves to be taken seriously, for there is a tendency to ascribe to new technology some magical quality taking it altogether beyond the plane of established legal principle.

This paper is concerned with two question arising from the use of EFT as an instantaneous settlement system:[1] when does a payment instruction or undertaking communicated by automated EFT become irrevocable? and when is payment considered complete? My thesis is that on both these questions EFT does not so much raise legal issues peculiar to itself as highlight the remarkable lack of clear rules for determining the time of commitment and payment through any mechanism other than negotiable and non-negotiable instruments.

Setting the scene

For ease of exposition I shall concentrate on a single transaction involving six parties. D, who has taken a vessel on a charterparty, wishes to make a hire payment to the charterer, C. The charterparty provides that all hire payments are to be made to C's bank, CB, for C's account. D asks his own bank, DB, to arrange for funds to be transferred to cover the hire payment about to become due. Neither DB nor CB is a clearing bank. DB's clearing agent is X and CB's clearing agent is Y. Since D and C bank with different banks who have different clearing agents, no question of an in-house transfer of funds arises, and all settlements will go through the clearing.

---

1. For EFT as a deferred settlement system, see Professor Ellinger's paper, p29 *post.*

The transaction sets up a chain of communications and funds transfers which can be expressed in diagrammatic form as follows:

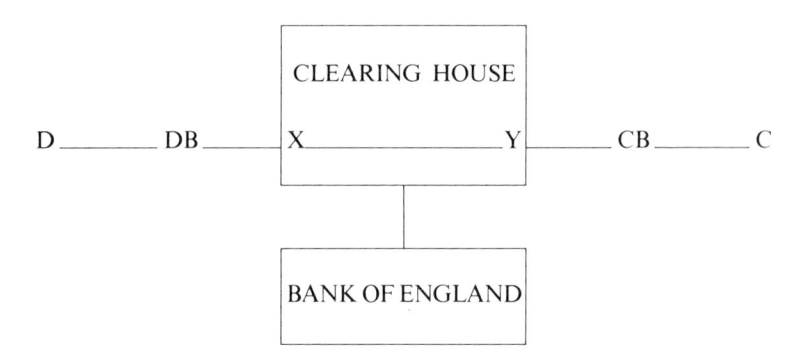

```
                    ┌─────────────────────┐
                    │  CLEARING HOUSE     │
D _____ DB _____  │X_____Y│ _____ CB _____ C
                    │         │           │
                    └─────────┼───────────┘
                              │
                    ┌─────────┴───────────┐
                    │                     │
                    │  BANK OF ENGLAND    │
                    │                     │
                    └─────────────────────┘
```

The direction of the flow of instructions depends on whether the payment takes the form of a credit transfer or a debit collection. A credit transfer is a 'push' of funds by the debtor to the creditor. D takes the initiative by instructing his bank, DB, to transfer the required sum to CB for the account of C. In this case, the instructions will flow from left to right in the above diagram, running from DB to CB via their respective clearing agents X and Y. A debit collection is a 'pull' of funds by the creditor from the debtor. Here C takes the initiative in collecting the money due to him, as by arranging for CB to collect on his behalf the amount of a cheque drawn by D on DB in favour of C or the amount of a direct debit voucher completed by C pursuant to D's prior authority. In this case, instructions will flow from right to left in the diagram, and again CB and DB will act through their respective clearing agents Y and X.

Some definitions

Descriptions of the funds transfer process are dogged by terminological imprecision and inconsistency. Since it is the privilege of any writer to create his own dictionary, let me begin by defining my terms, before going on to explore some of the issues raised by EFT in relation to the above transaction.

By *payment* I mean the transfer of funds or the performance of some other act which is effective to discharge a monetary liability. Since we are concerned with the discharge of obligations by a money transfer (as opposed, for example, to barter, part-exchange, combination of accounts or set-off), I shall confine my remarks to this form of payment; and since it is unusual to pay large amounts in cash, the method of payment I shall discuss in this paper is the transfer of a claim. Debtor and creditor agree, as in our example, that the debtor's obligation is to be discharged by procuring the conferment on C of an unconditional claim against his own bank, CB. D's claim against DB is reduced (or his liability to DB increased), whilst C's claim against CB is increased (or his liability to CB reduced), so that effectively D's net position with his bank deteriorates and C's net position against his bank improves by the same amount.

The transfer of funds is to be distinguished from a mere *commitment or undertaking* to make a transfer. Because a bank's word is generally considered to be not only as good as its bond but as the equivalent of cash, transfer and commitment to pay are often treated as synonymous. Since debtors and creditors frequently agree to accept a bank's undertaking to pay as amounting to conditional payment, the assumption that the undertaking constitutes payment is understandable enough, and in most cases nothing turns on the distinction. But the difference between payment and commitment to pay[2] becomes of profound importance in at least two cases. The first is where the bank giving the commitment becomes insolvent before discharging its obligations. In such a case the beneficiary of the bank's payment undertaking has no claim to any funds, merely a right to prove in the insolvency in competition with other creditors; and the creditor for whom the undertaking constituted conditional payment may assert his right to demand payment from the debtor. If the latter has already parted with his money, he will have to pay all over again. Such is the case where, for example, a bank issuing or confirming an irrevocable credit in favour of a seller after being put in funds by the buyer becomes insolvent before honouring the credit. The seller can then look to the buyer direct for payment of the price.[3] The second case where the distinction between commitment and payment is important is where the *receiving* bank becomes insolvent *after* payment. Here the

---

2. The two coincide where there has been a transfer of funds in anticipation of the payment instruction becoming irrevocable, as in the case of a cheque passed through the clearing. Here, expiration of the time allowed for revocation completes the payment.
3. *W. J. Alan & Co Ltd v El Nasr Export & Import Co* [1972] 2 All E R 127; *E. D. & F. Man v Nigerian Sweets & Confectionery Co Ltd* [1972] 2 Lloyd's Rep 50.

creditor has to bear the loss,[4] whereas if the bank were to become insolvent before the payment process had been completed the debtor would have to pay again.[5]

Payment is commonly preceded by an accounting stage which I shall refer to as *settlement*. Again, there is no consistent usage of the word 'settlement', which is sometimes treated as synonymous with payment, but I shall use this word to denote the striking of an agreed balance between accounting parties engaged in mutual dealings pursuant to which their respective monetary obligations towards each other are reflected by debit and credit entries in a current account. Settlement in this sense denotes what English contract lawyers call an *account stated*, an agreed balance without need to rely on the original consideration for the individual items making up the account. Settlement fixes the balance to be paid but, like any other form of commitment, does not itself constitute payment. This does not come about until funds are transferred.

The distinction between settlement and payment is clearly brought out in the settlement process of the Bankers' Clearing House. At the end of the day, inter-bank debits and credits are netted out (based either on that day's dealings or on those of the previous day, according to the particular clearing involved), so that some clearing banks end up as creditors and others as debtors. The establishment of the net balances in the clearing house is what constitutes settlement. Payment by a debtor bank to a creditor bank takes place only when funds are transferred by entries in the accounts of the two banks with the Bank of England as the central bank. Again, the distinction between settlement and payment is of little significance except in the unlikely event of failure of a clearing bank, or of a non-clearing bank for whom

---

4. See *Royal Products Ltd v Midland Bank Ltd* [1981] 2 Lloyd's Rep 194, where the plaintiffs directed that funds be transferred from an account with the defendants to an account in their name with a third bank, and when the latter became insolvent sought unsuccessfully to claim *inter alia* that the payment process had not been completed.
5. See *Re Farrow's Bank* [1923] 1 Ch 41, where a bank, having received a cheque for collection and passed it through to its clearing agents for collection, became insolvent. It was held that at the time of the insolvency the transfer of funds to the bank, and therefore to the customer, had not been completed, with the result that the proceeds of the cheque collected by the clearing agents after the bank's insolvency belonged to the customer and did not form part of the failed bank's assets in respect of which the customer would have been restricted to a right of proof in competition with other creditors.

it acts as clearing agent. In the absence of any valid clearing house rule to the contrary, failure of a debtor clearing bank means that its creditor banks are left to prove as unsecured creditors in its winding up (assuming no other method of recovery, such as set-off), whilst failure of a non-clearing bank leaves its clearing agent in the position of having to honour its commitments in the clearing entered into on behalf of the non-clearer, with a right of proof against the non-clearer in respect of the agent's right of indemnity when it has discharged its obligations.

Commitment to pay and payment through tangible payment methods

As a prelude to 'pure', ie automated or computer-to-computer, EFT, it is instructive to look at the present state of the law (so far as we can ascertain it) on commitment and payment under methods of transfer using paper-based or magnetic instructions. Of the many issues that can arise, I shall discuss two only, namely:

When does a payment instruction or undertaking become irrevocable? and
When is payment (in the sense of funds transfer) to be considered complete?

Each of these questions will be examined in the context of the transaction between D and C described earlier and illustrated in the diagram. When seeking to answer these questions it is important to have in mind the particular relationship that is under consideration. Thus there may be a transfer of funds from D to C even though no funds have passed from DB to CB. Conversely, CB may have received funds from DB but not yet made these available to C.

(i) When is a payment instruction or undertaking irrevocable?

Principal becomes committed when agent becomes committed
One who instructs another to pay money to a third party impliedly agrees to reimburse the paying party and, as a corollary, becomes committed to the paying party from the moment the latter incurs a commitment to the third party.[6] So in our

---

6. *Warlow v Harrison* (1859) 1 E & E 709; *Walker v Rostron* (1842) 9 M & W 41: *Griffin v Weatherby* (1868) L R 3 QB 753.

19

example, D, having instructed DB to remit funds to CB for the account of C, ceases to be able to cancel the instruction at the point where DB becomes committed to its own agent, X, which in turn is when X becomes committed to Y.

Up to this point, the timing of the commitments is in symmetry, for DB acts under a mandate from D, whilst X acts under a mandate from DB, so that the three parties are all on the same side, as it were, ie the paying side. However, it does not follow that X's commitment to Y is dependent on Y's being committed to CB. X and Y are not on the same side and their relationship is not that of principal and mandatory. The dealing between them in the clearing constitutes an item in the overall inter-bank settlement affecting not only X and Y but all other banks involved in the clearing, whether as clearing agents or as other banks or institutions operating through clearing agents. Hence the possibility that X becomes committed to Y irrespective of whether Y has yet incurred a commitment to CB.

Specific cases
With these preliminary observations, we can look at a series of alternative payment methods not involving automated EFT, in order to see how EFT might change the ground rules.

(1) *Bills, cheques and other instruments*
Where payment is by bill, cheque or other instrument, the rule is tolerably clear (indeed, as will be seen, this is one of the few cases where it is clear). If D draws a cheque on DB in favour of C and this is passed through the clearing,[7] X becomes committed to Y, and DB to X, etc, when Y is informed (whether before or after presentation of the cheque) that the cheque will be paid or DB fails to return the cheque within the time laid down by the clearing house rules.[8]

7. In the case of in-house transfers, ie where D and C bank at the same branch of the same bank, the bank becomes committed to pay at the moment it recognises C as its creditor instead of D, irrespective whether C's account has actually been credited. In this case, commitment to pay and payment coincide. If D and C bank at different branches, the two branches are treated for most purposes as if they were separate banks, though of course no clearing is involved. See R. M. Goode, 'When is a Cheque Paid?' [1983] JBL 164.
8. In general, the item must be returned unpaid the same day, but in the case of the General Clearing there is an extension to the next working day (on the telephone by noon, for sums in excess of £30) where the need to return an article through lack of funds, countermand of payment, etc, has not been noticed due to inadvertence on the day of presentation (General Clearing Rules, Rule (12)(b)).

(2) *Paper-based direct debit*[9]

Where C is to collect payment from D by direct debit and arranges for CB to put the direct debit through the clearing, at what point does X become committed to Y so as to make D's direct debit authority for the payment irrevocable? Since a direct debit voucher is in practice treated in the same way as a cheque, one presumes that the same rules apply, though true to their cryptic formulation the Clearing House Rules contain no reference whatsoever to direct debits! The one major difference between a direct debit voucher and a cheque is that the indemnity given by C to DB as a condition of DB agreeing to act on C's instructions enables DB to recover (and thus by inference to stop at any time before it has been made) a payment to which C was not entitled.

(3) *Direct debit through BACS*

If the position with paper-based direct debits is not entirely clear, it is positively obscure in the case where C or CB submits the direct debit in magnetic form through the Bankers' Automated Clearing Services. The general understanding among banks operating BACS is said to be that a payment instruction can be recalled at any time prior to the time of opening of the receiving branch following overnight notification of the transfer to that branch by its bank's sorting office, provided that the recall comes in time for the BACS system to reverse the debit and credit entries. This to some extent leaves the point of ultimate commitment to the discretion of the BACS systems management. But if the above correctly states the position, it means that a payment instruction sent through BACS can be recalled when the magnetic tape, disk, etc, embodying it is on the way to BACS or when it is at BACS and the item is being transferred to the BACS tapes or when the sorted items on the BACS tapes leave BACS for the sorting offices of the paying and collecting banks or even after that, when the transfer of the instructions from the sorting offices to the relevant branches is under way. It is questionable whether banking practice is sufficiently widespread or established to be regarded as a rule which the courts will necessarily accept. Once again, much is made to depend on the uncodified practice of bankers.

(4) *Credit transfer*

Similar uncertainty surrounds the credit transfer. Does a paper-based credit transfer become irrevocable when received by Y in the clearing, when received by CB, when notified by CB to C or

---

9. Now largely replaced by BACS.

on conclusion of the Daily Settlement? The answer is that we do not know. It appears to be the case that a special credit transfer or other payment undertaking, such as a banker's payment, sent by DB direct to CB instead of being passed through the clearing binds DB when received and accepted by CB.[10] But where it goes through the clearing there is no rule. Surprisingly, the Credit Clearing Rules do not cover the point at all. They deal with the return of 'Wrongly Delivereds' but not with credit transfers correctly issued and routed. Where the credit transfer is through BACS it becomes irrevocable at the same time as a BACS direct debit – if one only knew when that was!

(ii) When is payment complete?
The answer to this question involves identifying the time at which funds are actually transferred from D to C. This has no necessary connection with the time at which funds are transferred between the parties' banks. C may receive payment before, when or after CB has been put in funds by DB through X and Y.

As between D and C, what constitutes payment depends on the contract between them and on CB's actual or ostensible authority, first, from C to accept a tender of payment and, secondly, from DB or X to make the payment. Assuming that the agreed machinery of payment is a transfer of funds by D to CB to the credit of C's account, the channel of communication used to produce this result – in particular, the use of one or more banks as intermediaries between D and CB – is a matter of indifference to C, so long as he receives net the sum to which he is entitled. In general, we can say that C is paid at the moment when, with the actual or ostensible authority of DB or its agent, C acquires an unconditional claim against CB for the amount in question, ie when:

(1) CB, whether or not itself in funds from DB, pays or credits C with the actual or ostensible authority of DB or X, or

(2) CB, without such authority and whether or not in funds from DB, pays or credits C purportedly on behalf of DB or X, who subsequently ratifies such payment, or

(3) CB, having actual or ostensible authority to accept payment on behalf of C, accepts a transfer of funds for C's account, or

(4) CB, without such authority, accepts a transfer of funds on C's behalf and C subsequently ratifies the acceptance,

---

10. See *Momm v Barclays Bank International Ltd* [1977] QB 790.

and in each case the payment, credit or transfer is or has become unconditional. Where CB, without actual or ostensible authority to do so, pays or credits C, this is not a payment of D's debt to C – for the unauthorised payment of another's debt is ineffective in law – but amounts to no more than an advance by C from its own funds.

Automated electronic funds transfer

Against this background we can attempt to assess the impact of automated EFT on existing legal rules as to commitment to pay and payment. As I have endeavoured to show, whilst the rules on payment are tolerably clear (though hard to extract from the cases), there is a good deal of uncertainty as to the time when a payment instruction or undertaking not embodied in a cheque or other instrument becomes irrevocable. Does EFT raise additional considerations? Again, it is necessary to distinguish commitment to pay from payment.

(i) Commitment to pay
Where this is governed by a Clearing House rule, no great problem arises. Thus under the CHAPS rules a payment instruction routed through the appropriate gateway becomes irrevocable as soon as the payee settlement bank sends the payer settlement bank a 'logical acknowledgement'. The effect of such an act is to bind the payer bank to transfer the funds and the payee bank to give same-day value to its payee customer,[11] as well as binding all other settlement banks.[12] The question is more troublesome where there is no Clearing House rule. The uncodified custom of banks may help there, but it takes time for a practice to gain general acceptance. If the court has to formulate its own rule without the benefit of evidence as to the existence of such a custom, its problem is that other payment mechanisms do not appear to have thrown up any discernible principle from which a new rule may be fashioned. It is interesting to find that the same is true in the United States. Professor Hal Scott, when writing about the draft Uniform New Payments Code, comments:

'Ironically, however, the payment system transferring the

---

11. Rule (4)(c). Unresolved is the question whether CB, having given same-day value to C, can debit this back if DB fails to honour its commitment.
12. Rule (4)(d). Whether the Clearing House Rules bind C and D is another matter.

23

greatest value is governed by a poorly developed framework of legal rules. Other non-cash systems such as checks and credit cards are governed by a comprehensive body of statutory law or private contractual arrangements. However, due to a lack of statutory coverage and the limited use and scope of private contracts, only a fragmented body of common law governs wire transfers. This anomaly in the law of commercial transactions is a matter of substantial concern to the banking community. It also creates the risk that the courts will lack adequate guidance in deciding cases in this uncharted area and increases unnecessarily the uncertainties and risks faced by the parties to wire transfers.'[13]

The formulation of a rule may depend in some measure both on the system and on the detail of new technology.

Unitised transfers and batching
Where, as in CHAPS, payment instructions are transmitted by bilateral communication between banks, transmission and receipt of a payment message are almost instantaneous. The position of the transferor bank and the transferee bank is no different in essence from what it is under the more traditional near-instantaneous methods of communication such as the telephone and the telex. Both banks can monitor their respective positions at such frequency as they choose. But if the volume of inter-bank transfers reaches a level that cannot be accommodated by a network of bilateral transmission, so that an automatic clearing house (ACH) becomes necessary as a sorting and switching centre, a new factor is introduced, in that such a system involves a significant period of processing and batching in the ACH before the payment messages are routed to their various destinations. Thus BACS completes its processing overnight at the end of day 1 of the cycle, and there is a similar overnight processing at the end of day 2 by each bank when sorting and preparing the lists of items to be transferred to its branches in readiness for opening on day 3. During this batching period, the participating banks do not have a fully accurate picture of how they stand in relation to each other. This was exemplified in the *Herstatt* case,[14] where Barclays

---

13. 'Corporate Wire Transfers and the Uniform New Payments Code', 83 Col L. Rev 1664 (1983). In England, there is not only a dearth of case law and contractual arrangements but also an almost total lack of legal literature. The fullest treatment is to be found in Pennington, Hudson & Mann, *Commercial Banking Law*, pp 291 *et seq*; Anu Arora, 'Future Developments in Money Transfer' [1981] LMCLQ 56; and R. M. Goode, *Payment Obligations in Commercial and Financial Transactions*, Chapters I, IV.
14. *Supra*, n 10.

Bank, believing that Herstatt's account was in credit, initiated a substantial in-house transfer of funds to another customer at Herstatt's request, only to discover the following morning that Herstatt's account was substantially in debit. It then reversed the entries, a step held by Kerr J. to be ineffective, since payment was complete from the moment the computer process to effect the transfer was set in motion. Even the few hours' exposure involved in overnight processing or same-day settlement is potentially huge, and it is no doubt this fact that led the New York Clearing House to provide a measure of reversibility in its CHIPS Rules to cover the case of a participating (non-clearing) bank failing to honour its commitments to its settling (clearing) bank agent. Since the effect of an 'unwind' under the CHIPS Rules where such failure occurs is to eliminate all the transfers from and to the defaulting participant by deleting these from the inter-bank settlement,[15] the complications must be horrendous.

Breakdown or delay in communication
Just as the courts have had to consider what happens if there is a failure of or delay in communication through telex – eg because the message arrives after the recipient bank has closed up for the night or because the telex machine receiving the message has run out of paper or the equipment has jammed[16] – so also there may be breakdown or delay in the delivery of a computer-to-computer message. Automated EFT does not seem to raise any special problems here, except in terms of responsibility for the functioning and security of the system.

(ii) Payment
There seems no reason why automated EFT should in any way affect the rules as to the time when payment is completed through a transfer of funds. Insofar as payment by CB to C depends on CB's receipt of money through, say, an inter-bank transfer between X and Y, the sole effect of EFT is to accelerate the process.

CB's ability to refuse a payment tendered through DB and X on behalf of C is in no way lessened by EFT. As the law stands at the moment, a bank's receipt of money for its customer is *prima facie*

---

15. CHIPS Rules, paras 13b, 13d.
16. So far, there has been no case directly in point and the judicial pronouncements have all been *obiter dicta*. See, for example, the speech of Lord Wilberforce in *Brinkibon Ltd v Stahag Stahl und Stahlwarenhandlesgesellschaft mbH* [1983] 2 AC 34 at p 42; and N. Kasiraja, 'Contract by Telex – When is it Formed?' (1984) 26 Malaya L. Rev 168.

a purely ministerial act and does not of itself constitute acceptance by the customer.[17] In fact, EFT may make it easier to prevent an unwanted receipt altogether, for the system can be programmed to reject a transfer instruction which C has told CB not to accept.

Conclusions

For the most part, legal problems arising from EFT are not peculiar to the mechanism of payment but reflect the lack of any general formulation of rules as to commitment and payment, whether by the banking community or by the courts. Enquiry of experienced bankers is likely to extract little more than the comment that so far no real problems have arisen and that the transferor and transferee banks are usually able to reach an amicable agreement on the recall of payment instructions without the need for any guiding principle or legal rule.

Of course, this works well enough where nothing very much turns on the question whether the payment instruction initiated by D has passed the point of no return. But in many cases the banks' accounting processes are such that C may never know there was a moment at which CB held in its hands a credit transfer for C's account or had received an electronic signal notifying an amount to be paid. In the *Herstatt* case[18] it was not until discovery that the plaintiffs became aware of the fact that sums had been credited to their account one day and debited back the next morning when the computer printout showed that the defendant bank was uncovered in its account with Herstatt. So at least one question raised both by inter-bank transfers and by in-house transfers is the customer's awareness of what has gone on. Another, common to all payment systems, is the extent to which inter-bank agreements as to commitment and payment bind the banks' non-banking customers. No doubt customers may in general be taken to contract with reference to reasonable bank custom and usage, including custom and usage codified in clearing house rules. If this is so, it must presumably follow that they are entitled to complain if two banks agree between themselves to relax or waive the rules, eg by allowing an item to be recalled when under clearing house rules or established banking practice it had ceased to be recallable. And if there are no established rules, the question when an item is recallable cannot be left solely to the discretion of the two banks concerned.

17. *Mardorf Peach & Co Ltd v Attica Sea Carriers Corp of Liberia* [1977] AC 850.
18. *Supra*, n 10.

What is evident is that one of these days the questions of commitment and payment will arise in acute form in an inter-bank transaction involving large sums of money, and protracted and costly litigation is likely to result. There is surely much to be said for the banks taking the initiative in formulating clear and acceptable rules which fairly balance the legitimate requirements of bankers in an electronic age and those of their customers, the rules being incorporated by express reference in written contracts in the same way as for the Uniform Customs and Practice for Documentary Credits. If litigation does occur, then at least it is the banking community itself that will have had a chance to influence the outcome.

ELECTRONIC FUNDS TRANSFER AS A DEFERRED SETTLEMENT SYSTEM

Peter Ellinger

The objective of this paper is to review two questions which, though conceptually quite separate, are linked by technological considerations. They relate to the making of deferred payment undertakings by means of EFT networks.

The first problem is whether such arrangements are currently feasible. In other words, can a debtor utilise an EFT in the same way as a document in order to enter into a deferred payment undertaking. There is, of course, an endless variety of deferred payment undertakings executed on paper. They include all types of contracts, such as leases, hire-purchase agreements, IOUs and certain types of negotiable instruments. It will be shown that EFTs are not used for these purposes at present.

The second problem discussed in this paper is the future of negotiable instruments in the light of the advent of EFTs. The paper concentrates on bills of exchange and on promissory notes, as cheques, which are not covered, are issued for the immediate settlement of obligations. The question to be asked is whether bills of exchange and promissory notes may be taken over by deferred payment EFTs. For the purposes of this discussion it will, of course, be necessary to study the basic attributes of these instruments. It may be said at the outset that their unique characteristics would pose a challenge to any EFT network that wished to make provision for them by the use of its technology.

It is important to emphasise a fundamental distinction between the two subjects here discussed. The feasibility of using an EFT network for a deferred payment undertaking is a topical problem. The means are available but the question is how to put them into operation. The replacement of bills of exchange and promissory notes by records stored by an EFT network appears at this stage a plan for the future. This, though, is not a reason for dismissing the subject. The existence of independent EFT networks would have looked just as far-fetched half a century ago.

In discussing the two subjects, it is essential to concentrate on binding undertakings. The point is explained by reflecting on a cheque. As between the bank on whom the cheque is drawn and the holder, the cheque does not constitute an undertaking. The bank, which is merely the customer's agent, has the authority to honour the cheque,[1] but, in terms of the instrument, the bank is not under an obligation to make payment. Indeed, if the bank receives notice of countermand before it pays the instrument, it is bound to dishonour it.[2] The customer's (drawer's) position is different. Despite the stop-order, he remains liable to pay the cheque to a holder in due course. When he issued the instrument, the customer warranted that the cheque would be met when presented to the bank.[3] The customer, therefore, undertook a payment obligation. As the payee may present a cheque to the bank at any time such an undertaking is not, however, a 'deferred payment obligation'.

The distinction, then, is between a party's authority to pay and an actual duty or undertaking to do so. A party cannot usually be sued by a person to whom he has been asked, or been authorised, to pay money. The exceptions are to be found in the assignment of a debt,[4] and in the law of trusts. In the latter case, equity imposes certain duties on the trustee. In the former case, the assignment vests the debt in the assignee. Subject to certain exceptions,[5] the assignee is given the right to demand payment. But the mere beneficiary of a contract, made for his benefit between two other parties, remains a bystander. He does not have any contractual rights. It will be shown that this point is of major importance as regards payment arrangements of current EFT networks.

EFT networks and deferred payments

The transfer of money by means other than negotiable instruments is no novelty. Telegraphic transfers and transfers by telex have been known for a number of decades. They have superseded the mail transfer system. This paper, though, is concerned with EFT networks. Individual transfers such as by t/t or by telex, are unlikely to provide the means for deferred payments EFTs.

At present there are three EFT networks in the United Kingdom: BACS, CHAPS and SWIFT. BACS is maintained by a com-

---

1. *London Joint Stock Bank v Macmillan and Arthur* [1918] AC 777.
2. The Bills of Exchange Act 1882 (the 'BEA'), s75(1); and see *Westminster Bank v Hilton* (1926) 136 LT 315.
3. BEA, s55(1).
4. See, generally, *Chitty on Contracts*, 25th ed, Vol 1, Chap 19.
5. Such as the need of joining the assignor as party to proceedings, in certain types of equitable assignment; ibid §1289.

pany owned by the clearers. CHAPS is a network which utilises the services provided by a system of British Telecommunications. SWIFT is an international network, with a worldwide operation. A brief description of the three existing networks will throw light on the problems incurred by them in respect of deferred payment transfers.[6]

BACS
BACS is in reality a clearing house for credit transfers. The procedure is best illustrated by using as an example a series of payments made directly between two banks. The transferring bank prepares a tape, which sets out the relevant items to be transmitted. The details include the name of the customer who has instituted the transfer, the amount, and details concerning the payee and his account. The tape is delivered to BACS's headquarters at Edgware. At this clearing house, the tape, which is arranged on the basis of the identity of the payors, is electronically converted into tapes based on the identity of the recipient banks and the payees. The converted tapes are sent out by messenger to the clearing departments of the recipient banks, where they are duly processed.

The process is somewhat modified in the case of 'sponsored customers', who are enabled, under the authority of one of the participating banks, to dispatch their tapes directly to BACS, sending a duplicate to the sponsoring bank. Many financial institutions and secondary banks, who are not members of the clearing house, operate in this way. BACS is used mainly in order to make regular payments, such as wages and rentals. Payment instructions are placed by the transferring bank on a tape when the amounts are due.

CHAPS
CHAPS is an entirely different type of system. Unlike BACS, which uses a three-day clearing cycle, CHAPS is a system meant for the same day settlement of accounts of no less than £10,000.[7] The system is, again, used by the clearers; but it is expected that eventually its use will become more widespread than that.

CHAPS operates through gateways (not a central computer centre like BACS). Each major participant has his own gateway

---

6. For a fuller explanation of the system see Goode, *Payment Obligations in Commercial and Financial Transactions*, London 1983, Chap IV.
7. The development of the system is vividly described by Clark, 'CHAPS – A New Approach to Payment Systems', April 1982, (Report prepared for IBRO).

and some of the smaller banks share one. Each participant can link his own branches to his gateway by a computer system of his choice. Approved customers can have their own direct link to their bank's gateway. To some of them, though, this presents problems. The systems used by the different participants are not compatible. A customer who maintains accounts with more than one participating bank is, thus, faced with the expense of having to purchase a number of computer systems in order to link himself to the gateway of each of his banks.[8] As a result, many continue to use the somewhat antiquated system of bankers' payments which, unlike CHAPS, is confined to settlements made within the City.[9]

A CHAPS payment is transferred as follows. From the branch which receives the customer's instruction, a message goes out to the gateway. From there it is transmitted through the British Telecom switching service (PSS), which is a nationwide network, to the gateway of the recipient bank. Under the CHAPS rules, the actual transfer is considered payment. It is not merely an advice that payment is to be executed. To effect transfer on the same day, the message must reach the transferring bank by 3.00 pm, except that a customer linked to his bank's gateway may deliver the message up to 3.45 pm.

SWIFT

Unlike BACS and CHAPS, which are domestic EFT networks, SWIFT is an international system.[10] It has three centres, situated in Brussels (the Head Office), in Amsterdam and Culpepper, Va, in the United States. The nature of the network is well explained by its full name: 'Society for Worldwide Interbank Financial Telecommunications'. As it is a network, utilised by the banking community as a whole, its function is not confined to EFTs. Letters of credit and other messages can be communicated through it. In reality, SWIFT is a communications network resembling PSS. When a bank receives a SWIFT transfer

---

8. A solution is being investigated. It is expected that either a software of a hardware package will perform the function of making each computer system compatible with the different gateways it has to use. The banks refrained from using a uniform system to avoid antitrust, or trade practices, problems.
9. Note that the American equivalent is known as: CHIPS.
10. For a vivid description of the system see Lingl, 'Risk Allocation in CHIPS and SWIFT' 22 *Harv L Rev* 621 (1980). See also Baker, 'SWIFT', 17 *Jo World Trd L* 458 (1983).

message, it has to decide whether or not to act on it.[11]

The actual mechanics of SWIFT are simple. Where a customer instructs his bank to transfer money by SWIFT, his message is transmitted to the national centre. If his bank has a SWIFT terminal, it will do so directly. Otherwise, it may have to use a telex communication to issue the transfer order to a correspondent, who has a terminal. The SWIFT centre (which in the UK is situated in the premises of BACS) takes the necessary steps to transmit the message to the recipient bank. However, if the recipient bank does not have a SWIFT terminal, the message will be sent to a participating bank, which will transmit it to the recipient bank. Thus, in the United States, the bank that receives the SWIFT message may use a CHIPS transfer. All SWIFT messages go through the main centres. A message from the United Kingdom will be transmitted through the Amsterdam centre.[12]

By now it should be clear that any payment effected through an EFT network involves at least four parties: the payor, the transferring bank, the recipient bank and the payee. In addition, there can be two intermediary banks. The payor may use a bank that is not linked to the required network and which, accordingly, will use the services of an appropriate correspondent. Similarly, the payee's bank may not be linked to the network and the message may, accordingly, be transmitted through another intermediary. Moreover, up to five separate means may be used to effect transfer. The payor in London may issue his order in writing; his bank may send a telex to its correspondent, who will then effect transfer by SWIFT. The recipient station may notify the payee's bank by means of another network (such as CHIPS in the USA) and the last mentioned bank may advise its customer, the payee, in writing or by telegram. Undoubtedly, such a variety of methods is far more likely to be used in international than in domestic transactions. But even in a CHAPS or BACS transfer there may be need for the interposition of a correspondent.

It is clear that the existing complexity of the EFT networks poses obstacles for the establishment of a deferred payments system. There can be no doubt that such a system would be useful. Thus, a charterer, faced with the need of making prompt pay-

---

11. By way of contrast, a CHAPS message, being equivalent to payment, has to be acted upon; this is the arrangement between the participating banks.
12. It is clear that problems arise due to the time differential. Messages are stored at the centre at the end of a business day.

33

ment of all rentals due from him, would find it best to utilise a method that ensured right at the outset that funds would be credited to the shipowner's bank account by the agreed times. A survey of British banks suggests that such an arrangement is not easily made at present. Most banks interviewed prefer to make a diary entry concerning the payments to be made on behalf of their customer (the charterer, in the illustration) and then effect the required transfers at the appropriate times, making allowances for delays.

The legal nature of EFTs

A brief analysis of the legal nature of EFTs and of the relationships between the parties thereto will explain the reasons for the British banks' policy. As most of the reported cases concern the question of the 'time of payment' and 'time for revocation', and are therefore covered in another paper,[13] it will be adequate to discuss the main principles.

EFTs and negotiable instruments
An EFT involves a string of contracts, none of which purports to bring into existence a negotiable instrument. This is so even if an electronic recording could be deemed 'writing' within the meaning of the BEA.[14] First, a negotiable instrument is payable to the payee's order. This means that the payee can determine (by transfer and negotiation) to whom the instrument is to be paid.[15] Secondly, an EFT, or even a manual giro credit, does not assume on its face the form of an unconditional order. Basically, the relevant EFT forms set out only the very details needed to effect transfer. These are also conveyed in the inter-bank handling of the transaction.

Thirdly, there is a practical distinction between a negotiable instrument and an EFT. A negotiable instrument is in itself the subject of transfer or negotiation. Each indorsement is completed by delivery.[16] Thus, one piece of paper passes from hand to hand. The EFT, be it a SWIFT, a CHAPS or a BACS transfer, involves a string of requests. The means for transmission is an electronic instruction; not a given piece of paper which has special attri-

---

13. See Prof. Goode's paper *ante,* p15.
14. Required under s3(1).
15. See the definition of a negotiable instrument in s3(1) and consider s8.
16. See ss31(2)–(3) and 21.

butes. It can be safely concluded that EFTs do not constitute negotiable instruments.

EFTs and assignments
It is equally safe to conclude that an EFT does not involve an assignment. This is so despite a view to the contrary expressed in some American authorities.[17] In English law, an EFT cannot be regarded as a statutory assignment within section 136 of the Law of Property Act 1925. First, it usually involves the transfer of only part of the chose in action (or debt) owed by the transferring bank to its customer, the payor.[18] Secondly, the order may not even relate to funds already accrued to the customer; it may be an order for a periodic payment to be executed if the customer's account has the required funds at the relevant period.

These considerations do not rule out the possibility of treating an EFT as an equitable assignment. But a practical consideration shows that no assignment is involved. When a customer gives his bank a 'standing order' it is understood that this may be stopped or modified at any time. In point of fact, a request to effect a transfer of any type can, in the very least, be countermanded before its execution. An equitable assignment, on the other hand, is complete by the time it is notified to the debtor (the bank in an EFT).[19]

The agency relationship
In reality, an EFT is simply an instruction given by a customer to his bank for the transfer of an amount of money to the payee. All the banks in the transaction act, therefore, in a representative capacity. This view was expressed in *Royal Products Ltd v Midland Bank Ltd* by Webster J.:[20]

> '(EFTs) are to be regarded simply as an authority and instruction, from the customer to the bank, to transfer an amount standing to the credit of that customer with that bank to the credit of his account with another bank ...'[21]

17. *Williams v Atlantic Assurance Co* [1933] 1 KB 1.
18. In the United States, see: *Delbrueck v Manufacturers' Hanover Trust Co*, 609 F 2d 1047, 1051 (1979); cf *Bayly, Martin & Fay Inc v Kenny*, unreported, 80 Civ 82–CSH of 18 February 1982. Note that the English case, *Rekstin v Severo Sibirsko Gosudarstvennoe Akcionerno* [1933] 1 KB 33, was decided on special facts. See *Chitty on Contracts*, 25th ed 1983, §§1276, 2652.
19. It may be complete even earlier than this, ie when executed. And see, generally, *Chitty on Contracts*, 25th ed 1983, §§1280, 2655.
20. [1981] 2 Lloyd's Rep 194, 198. His Lordship concluded that a duty of care to the customer was therefore owed by the bank. See also *Evra Corporation v Swiss Bank Corporation* 522 F Supp 820 (1981).
21. Or to the account of another customer.

The existence of such a string of agency relationships leads to a number of conclusions which will be shown to be of relevance as regards the introduction of deferred payment EFTs. First, although at common law an agent is answerable to his principal for the sub-agent's negligence,[22] there usually is an exclusion of such liability in the underlying contractual document.[23] This applies to contracts of EFT networks, except that some of them, such as SWIFT, will bear losses resulting from malfunctioning of their systems.

Secondly, in English law, there is no privity of contract between the principal and his agent's sub-agent.[24] This means that, where a transaction is governed by British law, the payor does not have an action in contract against any bank engaged by the transferring bank. The payee, in turn, has a right to bring an action in contract only against the recipient bank.

The position of the recipient bank is not quite certain. When it receives the funds, it acts initially on behalf of the transferring bank or the latter's correspondent. The recipient bank remains the other bank's agent up to the moment at which the recipient bank decides to credit the funds to the payee's account. There may be situations in which the payee has instructed that the funds be not accepted on his behalf, as is the case where payment is made out of date under a charterparty that the payee wishes to cancel.[25] At a certain moment, though, the recipient bank decides either to remit the funds back or to hold them for the payee.[26]

---

22. *Equitable Trust Co of New York v Dawson Partners Ltd* (1927) 27 LlLR 49.
23. The clauses are valid: *Calico Printers' Association Ltd v Barclays Bank Ltd* (1930) 36 Com Cas 71, affd, ibid, 197. The clauses are believed to be reasonable within the meaning of s11 of the Unfair Contract Terms Act 1977 and hence unassailable under s2(2) thereof.
24. *Calico Printers' Association Ltd v Barclays Bank Ltd*, (supra); *Royal Products Ltd v Midland Bank Ltd*, (supra). But contrast as regards the law in the United States: *Evra Corporation v Swiss Bank Corporation, (supra)*. There is here an interesting question of the conflict of laws.
25. For examples, see *The Brimnes* [1975] QB 929; *Mardorf Peach Co Ltd v Attica Sea Carriers Corporation of Liberia* [1977] AC 850; *The Chikuma* [1981] 1 WLR 314.
26. This usually is the moment of payment. A detailed analysis of the authorities is outside the scope of this paper; but see: *Rekstin v Severo Sibirsko Gosudarstvennoe Ackionernoe* [1933] KB 47; *Singer v Yokohama Specie Bank*, 47 NYS 2d 881 (1944), revd on a different point: 48 NYS 2d 799 (1949); and see 85 NE 2d 984 (1949); *Guaranty Trust Co of New York v Lyon*, 124 NYS 2d 680 (1953); *Momm v Barclays Bank International Ltd* (1977) QB 790; *Delbrueck & Co v Manufacturer's Hanover Trust Co*, 609 F 2d 1047, esp 1051 (1979) (and note the vivid description in this case of CHIPS); *Royal Products Ltd v Midland Bank Ltd* [1981] 2 Lloyd's Rep 194.

The fact that an EFT involves the creation of strings of agency contracts in respect of each transaction has hindered attempts to use EFT networks for deferred payment undertakings. A particular obstacle is the difficulty of determining the exact moment at which the recipient bank becomes the payee's agent. In a deferred payment undertaking a bank has to know, right from the outset, to whom it owes an obligation.

Moreover, there is always the possibility of a bankruptcy of a correspondent or of an embargo disrupting ordinary transactions. In the former case, the receipt and retention of the money by the foreign correspondent, to whom it was remitted in order to render a deferred payment, would result in its being paid to the trustee in bankruptcy. In the latter case, the position would be unclear and the customer could lose money. This would happen if payments to the foreign payee were to continue to be made by the correspondent despite the payee's inability to perform his part of the bargain. The correspondent might, of course, be bound to make these payments under the applicable local law.

There is the further, practical, problem of the moment of payment. This is of particular importance in SWIFT transfers. One of the required details in such a transaction is the statement of a 'value date', on which the money transferred is to be made available to the payee. The view of the English banks is that, up to that very point of time, the instruction to pay may be revoked. The 'Swedish rule', applicable in Scandinavia and, apparently, in some other Continental jurisdictions, is that the funds cannot be recalled after their having reached the hands of the recipient bank, regardless of whether the 'value date' has arrived or not.[27] It is clear that a deferred payment instruction, given by an English bank in London to a Scandinavian bank in Oslo, can lead to disputes where the customer wishes to revoke his deferred payment instruction.

It should be added that, even in respect of the legal principle in point, the question is a tricky one. Thus, an application of the general principles of agency law tends to support the Swedish rule. Once the recipient bank has notified the payee that it holds the funds for him, it probably retains them as his agent. Whilst the recipient bank cannot release the funds before the value date, it may be equally precluded from remitting them back to the transferring bank.

---

27. The 'value date' and its significance were discussed by the House of Lords in *The Chikuma*, (*supra*).

Will EFTs be used for deferred payments?

Practical problems militate also against the arrangement for a deferred payment EFT through BACS and CHAPS. The latter network simply does not countenance it. Its very object is to arrange for the same-day transfer of large amounts. The former is believed to have the necessary facilities. Practical considerations, though, advocate against their use. If such instructions were to be accepted, banks would have to refuse to obey a customer's countermand. From a bank's point of view, it is distasteful to tell a customer that an instruction cannot be revoked although it has not been executed.[28]

It is, thus, unlikely that deferred payment EFTs, which constitute binding undertakings, will become popular in the near future. One transaction, involving a binding arrangement for a deferred payment EFT is, however, universally recognised. This is the 'forward exchange contract', under which a customer agrees to purchase or to sell foreign currency at an agreed future date but at a rate that is agreed upon forthwith. The transaction, though, is one between the customer and his own bank. It, therefore, falls into an entirely different class.

It may be added that the current arrangements for warranting payments of amounts due on a deferred basis seem to work satisfactorily. In inland transactions, the secured loan and overdraft have adequate teeth to induce a debtor to pay. Additional security is available by means of a bank guarantee. Such a facility is at least as effective as deferred payment EFTs. In the overseas trade, the functions can also be performed by a guarantee but the most popular instrument is the documentary credit. Furthermore, an effective way to arrange for deferred payments is provided by the use of negotiable instruments. The prime instrument is the bill of exchange but, promissory notes, too, continue to play a role.

Will EFTs replace negotiable instruments?

Electronic transmission of bills of exchange
The question to be dealt with is not whether a negotiable instru-

---

28. Note that there are no difficult legal problems as a principal (payor) may give his agent (bank) an irrevocable payment instruction if the interests of a third party (payee) are dependent on it: Powers of Attorney Act 1971, s4(1) and, generally, *Bowstead on Agency*, 14th ed 1976, pp 423 et seq. For the common law position see *Smart v Sandars* (1848) 5 CB 895, 916–7.

ment may be electronically transmitted. There is no doubt that an EFT network can acquire the technology needed for this purpose. Some other forms of commercial paper, such as bills of lading, are currently produced and transmitted electronically.[29] Letters of credit, too, can be dispatched by 'teletransmissions'.[30] In terms of contents and details, negotiable instruments are less complex than either of these two documents.

The BEA does not preclude the dispatch of such instruments by an EFT network. Indeed, the definition of a bill of exchange in section 3(1) is wide enough to cover an instrument which is electronically transmitted. It is thought that a lithographed signature is adequate to meet the respective requisite of form of this section.[31] Moreover, an American authority took the view that a correctly worded telex message constituted a bill of exchange.[32] The District Court was not deterred by the fact that the 'signature' on the telex was teletransmitted.

It may thus, be possible to create a bill of exchange or promissory note by the use of an EFT network. But, once such an instrument reached its destination it would have to be treated as a document. To be used as a negotiable instrument, it would have to be transferred by indorsement and delivery; it would have to be presented for acceptance and for payment and, if dishonoured, might have to be protested. The advantage of transmitting a bill of exchange or a promissory note electronically is therefore limited.

The true question is whether such instruments may be replaced altogether by deferred payment EFTs of a negotiable character. Such an EFT would then be produced, transmitted, transferred and retired through the relevant network. The problems encountered in such a design are far more difficult than those related to the mere electronic transmission of traditional negotiable instru-

---

29. For an interesting discussion, see Davidson, 'UCP and Need for Amendments', in *Current Problems of Trade Financing*, Singapore 1983, 38, at pp 36 *et seq*.
30. Now recognised in the Uniform Customs and Practice for Documentary Credits, 1983 Revision, *ICC Brochure 400*, art 22(c). And see comment in 'UCP 1974/1983 Revisions Compared and Explained', *ICC Brochure 411*, p41.
31. *Ex p Birmingham Banking Co* (1868) LR 3 Ch App 651, 653–54; *Bird & Co v Thomas Cook & Son Ltd* [1937] 2 All ER 227. Note also that under s2, 'writing' includes 'printed'. By analogy, an electronically typed signature may, therefore, be properly written.
32. *Chase Manhattan Bank v Equibank*, 394 F Supp 352, 356 (1975), revd on a different point: 550 F 2d 882 (1977).

ments. Four legal problems would have to be solved before any attempts were made to introduce the required technological innovations. These are best understood if one considers the practical use of the major negotiable instrument – the bill of exchange.

Bills of exchange are used predominantly in the context of two facilities associated with international trade: the documentary credit (which is used exclusively in this context) and the acceptance credit (which is used in domestic projects as well). In the case of documentary credits, the seller usually draws a bill of exchange on the issuing or confirming bank for the amount of the credit. The bill, which may be payable at 90 or 180 days after sight, will be 'discounted' by the seller's own bank, who thereupon becomes the negotiating bank. This bank arranges for the presentment of the bill for acceptance and for payment, usually by engaging a correspondent.

The arrangement differs in an acceptance credit. Here an industrialist or manufacturer, who requires extra liquidity, may be unable to obtain a loan from his bank. But the bank may be prepared to lend him its credit. To do so, it authorises him to draw on itself bills of exchange for an amount not exceeding a stated ceiling. The bills are, thus, signed by the industrialist as drawer and by the bank as acceptor. The industrialist obtains his required finance by discounting the bill. He is able to arrange for this on the strength of the combined effect of the signatures of the bank and of himself.[33] The instrument may be discounted several times on the bills market. At maturity, it is met by the bank (the acceptor), which seeks reimbursement from the drawer. If the drawer is not in a position to settle, another set of bills is 'rolled over'.[34]

There are, of course, other transactions in which bills of exchange are being used. Thus, a bill accompanies c.i.f. documents transmitted by the seller of the goods to the purchaser. But in all the cases involved, the bill serves the same two objects. First, it purports to charge the person on whom it is drawn (the 'drawee'), whose consent to the demand ('acceptance') constitutes a deferred payment undertaking.[35] Secondly, the bill is meant to

---

33. For an excellent description of the practice see *The Bill on London*, published by Gillett Bros.
34. The question whether or not such an instrument is an accommodation bill, falls outside the scope of this paper.
35. BEA, ss 17 and 54.

be discounted. It therefore has to be negotiable which, for the present purpose, may be taken to mean: transferable by indorsement and delivery.[36]

Replacement of bills of exchange by EFT
The characteristics of bills of exchange foreshadow the problems that would have to be solved if they were to be replaced by deferred payment EFTs. The first and major one may be described as the contractual problem. Despite its terse and stereotyped text, a bill of exchange embodies a string of contracts. They are based on the undertaking assumed by each party. The acceptor promises to pay the instrument.[37] The drawer warrants that it will be both accepted and paid.[38] Any other person who transfers the instrument under his own signature – an indorser – assumes a similar undertaking.[39] Such an indorsement is often executed when a bill is re-discounted or, at the initial stages, to give it extra currency. If the bill is dishonoured by non-acceptance, an immediate right of recourse accrues to the 'holder' against the drawer and the indorsers.[40] If the accepted bill is dishonoured by non-payment, the holder has in addition the right to enforce the bill against the acceptor.[41] The 'holder' is the payee of the bill, its indorsee or the bearer, who has lawful possession of it.[42]

The bill of exchange thus constitutes a string of contracts. These are not only the contracts between the holder and the persons who have signed the bill in one or another capacity but also contractual relationships subsisting between those parties. Basically, each party has a right of recourse against earlier ones if the bill is not met.

It is difficult to see how such a string of contracts can be created by deferred payment EFTs. Even if one assumed that each party could add its signature to the bill by means of an electronic message, it remains difficult to see how this might accommodate the business world generally. Whilst most firms have access to computers, there is a great deal of incompatability between exist-

---

36. BEA, s31. Whether the transferree is a holder in due course (BEA, s29) and what are such a holder's rights (BEA, s38) are irrelevant questions in the present context).
37. BEA, s54.
38. BEA, s55(1).
39. BEA, s55(2).
40. BEA, s43(2).
41. BEA, s47(2).
42. BEA, s2.

ing hardware systems. It seems unlikely that all the participants in the bills market would have identical hardware. Moreover, usually the bill of exchange is physically transferred whenever it is indorsed and negotiated by a new party. Is an electronic bill to be moved from one computer terminal to another or is it to remain at its original location (eg the domicile bank) where each party's undertaking (viz 'signature') may be added to it?

The second problem regarding the creation of bills by deferred payment EFTs is based on the fact that a negotiable instrument needs to be transferable. This means that it must be of a type that may be indorsed and delivered.[43] There is no doubt that if the problem of 'signing' were solved it would be equally possible to transfer or deliver an electronically created bill by means of a teletransmission. Here, again, the harmonizing of hardware would be a prerequisite to the effective operation of a system.

The third obstacle to creating bills of exchange by means of deferred payment EFTs is related to the fact that a negotiable instrument constitutes an item of property and not just a string of contracts. This attribute of a bill is reflected by the importance played in respect of it by the concepts of possession and of property.

Thus, a person cannot be the holder of a bill unless he has its possession. In addition, a person can have a 'title' to a negotiable instrument.[44] If he loses a bill, he is entitled to a replacement.[45] Negotiable instruments are, thus, regarded as a special type of property. They differ from ordinary chattels in that their possession confers certain contractual rights on the holder. But they differ from contracts by the existence of the proprietary elements.[46]

This concept of negotiable instruments militates against their replacement by electronically created data records. Undoubtedly, the obstacles can be overcome. It is significant that abstract property rights, such as a trademark, a patent and a copyright, are universally understood and accepted. But the creation of a multi-party contract, which can be readily transferred, which confers property rights on its 'owner', and which is recorded by electronic means, remains a revolutionary concept.

43. BEA, ss31 and 21.
44. Thus, s79(2) BEA contemplates that a person may be the 'true owner' of a negotiable instrument. Also, a person deprived of it, has the right to bring an action in conversion.
45. BEA, ss69–70.
46. And see *R v Kohn* (1979) Crim L R 675.

The fourth and last objection may be best called the 'procedural difficulties'. A bill of exchange has to be presented for acceptance and for payment.[47] If it is dishonoured, the holder has to follow a certain procedure before he can bring actions to enforce his rights against the drawer and the indorsers.[48] He has to send notice of dishonour[49] and, in the case of a foreign bill,[50] has to effect protest through a notary.[51]

At present, it is difficult to envisage that all these procedures could be carried out by electronic means. To effect presentment, it would be necessary to ensure that all the relevant hardware systems were compatible. In that case, it would be possible to present bills by using a teletransmitted message. On the same basis, teletransmissions could be used for giving notice of dishonour only if all the recipients had the required terminals. Notarial protest – so dear to Continental practice – would have to be repealed or drastically modified.

The objections in question have been discussed with reference to bills. But they are equally relevant as regards promissory notes – in fact they are exacerbated in this case, as promissory notes are issued not only by businessmen. This means that the problem of harmonizing the hardware systems becomes insurmountable.

Even so, it is important to realise that the possibility of the replacement of traditional negotiable instruments by electronically produced and recorded data cannot be ruled out. It is possible to think in terms of a centre, in which such documents are recorded and stored, and which handles all the operations required in respect of them. Where required, it would arrange for discount, for presentment for acceptance and for payment and for the steps applicable on dishonour. There is no doubt that the BEA would have to be suitably amended to allow for such 'documents' and procedures.

Is deferred payment EFT necessary?
The last question to be asked is whether there is a need to replace traditional bills and notes by deferred payment EFTs. In the case of settlement instruments – such as cheques – the sheer daily

---

47. Otherwise, the drawer and indorsers are discharged: BEA, ss40(2), 45(1).
48. For a detailed discussion, see *Benjamin's Sale of Goods*, 2nd ed 1981, §§2092 et seq. The acceptor is liable even if the procedure is not observed: BEA, s52(3).
49. BEA, ss48–49.
50. Defined in BEA, s4.
51. BEA, s51.

volume called for the establishment of a network such as BACS. The need for speed and certainty fostered SWIFT and CHAPS. There is, of course, a volatile market of bills in London and elsewhere. The question, though, is whether its operation is so defective as to call for an expensive and fundamental reform.

PROCEDURE AND EVIDENCE:
The Maintenance of Transaction Records:
Proving the State of Account in EFT Transactions

Martin Karmel

EFTs are defined in s.903 (6) of the US Electronic Funds Transfer Act of 1978 as follows:

'The term "electronic funds transfer" means any transfer of funds, other than a transaction originated by check, draft, or similar paper instrument, which is initiated through an electronic terminal, telephonic instrument, or computer or magnetic tape so as to order, instruct, or authorise a financial institution to debit or credit an account. Such term includes, but is not limited to, point-of-sale transfers, automatic teller machines, direct deposits or withdrawals of funds, and transfers initiated by telephone.'

On the basis of that definition it is clear that there is no novelty in the idea or use of electronic funds transfers in day-to-day current account banking in the United Kingdom. For example, fully automated direct debits have been in use for the past fifteen years and automated teller machines for more than five years.

It is essential (and to the layman or the lay banker this is a difficult point to explain) to distinguish clearly in one's mind the basic difference between the purpose of the three statutes that are relevant to evidentiary issues.

On the one hand, there is the Bankers' Books Evidence Act 1879. This is an Act that deals with procedural issues only, and not with questions of admissibility as such. It relates to the 'Best Evidence Rule', ie since in the context of this paper the best evidence of a transaction is the book in which that transaction is entered then a copy of that book is not the best evidence. However, if the relevant parts of Barclays' books, say, had to be produced in their original form on the same day in separate courts in different parts of the country, then it would be anybody's guess which would collapse first, the business of the bank or the administration of justice. This, I have always understood, was the reason for this Act, which has nothing to do with hearsay evidence or the admissibility of the banker's book itself.

It is interesting to compare the side-notes to the BBEA with those to the Criminal Evidence Act and to the Civil Evidence Act. The relevant side-note in the BBEA is 'Mode of proof of entries in bankers' books' whilst those in the other two Acts contain the words 'admissible' and 'admissibility' *passim*. Equally, these words do not appear anywhere in the (extant parts of the) BBEA.

Continuing with the BBEA, it will be recalled that the 6th Schedule to the 1979 Banking Act extended the definition of a Banker's Book from the 1879 definition – 'ledgers, day books, cash books, account books and all other books used in the ordinary business of the bank' – by the addition of the following words 'whether those records are in written form or are kept on microfilm, magnetic tape or any other form of mechanical or electronic data retrieval mechanism'. Thus it follows that if an entry in a banker's book takes the form of a computer print-out, it is nevertheless still acceptable as evidence of an entry in the banker's book and, furthermore, by virtue of the provisions of section 10 of the 1879 Act it is evidence of such in both civil and criminal proceedings.

It is perhaps worth wondering in passing whether the words in the 6th Schedule were a *necessary* addition, other than on an 'avoidance of doubt' basis, bearing in mind the view expressed by Bridge, LJ in *Barker v Wilson*[1], that the BBEA 'must be construed in 1980 in relation to the practice of bankers as we now understand it. So construing the definition of "bankers' books" and the phrase "an entry in a banker's books", it seems to me that clearly both phrases are apt to include any form of permanent record kept by the bank of transactions relating to the bank's business, made by any of the methods which modern technology makes available, including, in particular, microfilm'. Incidentally, the Banking Act had not at that time yet come into effect.

By way of contrast, the Criminal Evidence Act 1965 and the Civil Evidence Act 1968 both relate to the admissibility in evidence of hearsay statements. However, it is interesting to observe that the Criminal Evidence Act does not actually mention the word 'computer' at all, nor is it phrased in the language or jargon of computery. Contrast this with s.5 of the Civil Evidence Act where the word 'computer' appears *passim*. One reason for this discrepancy presumably derives from the circumstances giving rise to the 1965 Act, namely the case of *Myers v DPP*[2], where the House of Lords held by a 3–2 majority that

1. [1980] 1 WLR 884.
2. [1965] AC 1001.

microfilmed records of the production cards which travel along the production line were not admissible evidence of the numbers of the component parts of particular motor vehicles. In the circumstances the workmen who had put the numbers on the cards could not be traced, and could clearly not have remembered particular combinations of numbers if they had been. That decision contained a plea from Lord Reid for legislation: 'The only satisfactory solution is by legislation following on a wide survey of the whole field, and I think that such a survey is overdue.'

One other reason for the difference in language may arise from the fact that no 'wide survey of the whole field' took place at that time, and one is entitled to try to cast one's mind back to 1965 to attempt to recall the usage of computers at that time. After all, how widespread were they and to what extent had they penetrated the public, let alone the judicial, consciousness? Was it not in the early 1950s that IBM had prophesied that the total world market for computers would be approximately thirty?!

The joker in the pack now is the Police and Criminal Evidence Act 1984 which has recently completed its passage through Parliament. Part VII – Documentary Evidence in Criminal Proceedings – of the Act, which has not yet fully come into force, will have the effect of repealing the Criminal Evidence Act in its entirety (and, rather mysteriously, section 82 of the County of Kent Act, 1981!). Part VII contains 5 sections only (68–72), section 69 reading as follows:

'69. (1) In any proceedings, a statement in a document produced by a computer shall not be admissible as evidence of any fact stated therein unless it is shown:
(a) that there are no reasonable grounds for believing that the statement is inaccurate because of improper use of the computer;
(b) that at all material times the computer was operating properly, or if not, that any respect in which it was not operating properly or was out of operation was not such as to affect the production of the document or the accuracy of its contents; and
(c) that any relevant conditions specified in rule of court under subsection (2) below are satisfied.

(2) Provision may be made by rules of court requiring that in any proceedings where it is desired to give a statement in evidence by virtue of this section such information concern-

ing the statement as may be required by the rules shall be provided in such form and at such time as may be so required.'

As previously mentioned, this Part of the Act is not yet in force, but the following may be noted:

(a) Part II of the Third Schedule strikes new statutory ground in an attempt to deal with the reliability of *input* to the computer. By way of contrast, section 5 of the Civil Evidence Act concerned itself solely with the possibility of the *output* being affected by technical malfunction.

(b) Section 69(2) presupposes that rules of court will be made to deal with the mechanics of the witness's supporting statement, presumably along the lines of Order 38, rule 24 in civil proceedings.

One incidental curiosity to be noted in this context is that the British Standards Institution has produced a standard (BS 6498:84) dealing with the preparation of microfilm and other microforms that may be required as evidence, with examples of certificates for use in connection with proceedings under both the Criminal Evidence Act and the Civil Evidence Act.

(c) The requirement in section 1(1) of the Criminal Evidence Act to the effect that the business records in question must relate to a trade or business and have been compiled in the course of that trade or business has not been carried through into section 69. Consequently, there no longer seems to be the risk – to which attention was drawn during the Bill's passage through Parliament – of printouts produced by investigating auditors being rejected as inadmissible under the sub-section on the grounds that they were prepared after the event and for the purpose of the prosecution rather than in the course of a trade or business (see *R. v Wood*[3]).

(d) It is arguable that Part VII of the Act can be seen as an edging away from the apparent complexities of the comparable provisions of the two previous Acts and as a move towards the Common Law position on the admissibility of evidence produced by mechanical instruments. This is set out in *Cross on Evidence* in the following terms:

'A presumption which serves the same purpose of saving the time and expense of calling evidence as that served by the maxim *"omnia praesumuntur rite esse acta"* is the presump-

---

3. (1983) 76 Cr App Rep 23.

tion that mechanical instruments were in order when they were used. In the absence of evidence to the contrary, the courts will presume that stopwatches and speedometers and traffic lights were in order at the material time; but the instrument must be one of a kind as to which it is common knowledge that they are more often than not in working order.'

That passage received the approval of the Divisional Court in *Castle v Cross*,[4] a case dealing with the admissibility of a printout of readings from an intoximeter device, where Stephen Brown, LJ accepted the argument that though an intoximeter was a sophisticated machine which depended for part of its operation upon computer control that did not set it in a different class from other sophisticated mechanical devices and instruments. That partial equation between a computer-produced printout and a reading from other devices and instruments may be significant for the future.

There are few reported cases of relevance, but in *R v Pettigrew*,[5] the question before the Court of Appeal was the admissibility under the Criminal Evidence Act of a printout of the serial numbers in a bundle of banknotes sent out by the Bank of England. Apparently the operator supplied information to the computer about the serial number of the first note printed in each bundle and thereafter the computer automatically produced a list of the numbers of the rejected notes. The Court of Appeal held that the computer output listing the numbers of the remaining notes in the bundles was inadmissible because the machine's operator did not have personal knowledge of the numbers of the rejected notes – the requirement in s.1(1)(a) of the Act had not been met because to be admissible in evidence the record had to be compiled from information supplied by a person with personal knowledge of the matters dealt with in the information supplied.

The views expressed by the Court of Appeal followed an argument by counsel which the members of the court found to be 'most effective'. However, that argument was not followed subsequently in *R v Wood*,[6] where a differently constituted court took the line that where a computer is used as a calculator (which was arguably what occured in *Pettigrew*) and its programming and use are both covered by oral evidence, the printout produced is not

---

4. [1984] 1 WLR 1372.
5. (1980) 71 Cr App R 39.
6. (*supra*).

hearsay evidence. A computer printout, it was held in that case, is not a statement made by a witness but should more properly be treated as a piece of oral evidence, the actual proof of evidence of which depends on the testimony of a witness. The computer was a tool and did not contribute to its own knowledge.

Even apart from the views expressed in *Wood* there is still some feeling of surprise that no attempt was made in *Pettigrew's* case to prove the operation of the machine under ordinary common law rules, and this feeling is reinforced by the dicta of Stephen Brown, LJ in *Castle v Cross* (*supra*). Nonetheless, at the end of the day there is the lingering suspicion that the Court of Appeal in *Pettigrew* was blinded by science into accepting a misconceived argument on behalf of the appellant.

So far this paper has addressed itself to formal evidentiary issues, but underlying these various formalities is to be found a question of more practical significance. This is the question of proof, which in this context means 'how do you prove (or disprove) the genuineness of an ATM transaction initiated by means of a personal identification number (PIN)?' In paper-based transactions dependent on a signature the matter of proof – which, it is repeated, is to be distinguished from the question of admissibility of evidence – will at the end of the day rest on the validity of a signature which is capable of being proved or disproved by expert evidence, whether it be that of a handwriting expert *simpliciter*, or of a similar expert operating an appropriate device. We are now, however, talking about a paperless and unsigned transaction and how a bank can prove that a PIN was put into the ATM by the genuine card-holder. Equally, how does the genuine card-holder prove that he has not told anybody his PIN and that no third party could have used his card?

That this is a matter of public concern is indicated by the following passage from the National Consumer Council's 1983 Report on Banking Services and the Consumer*:

> 'We are particularly concerned with ... [episodes involving the erroneous debiting of cards in apparently inexplicable circumstances]. On the 19th January 1981 the *Daily Mirror's* city editor, Mr Robert Head, published a selection of letters from readers who claim to have been the victim of some form of 'robotic theft'. (An unpublished file of letters was also kindly made available to us by Mr Head.) Total sums of between £5

---

*And see now the NCC's 1985 report *Losing at Cards* (ed.)

and £1,300 had been debited from correspondents' accounts following alleged withdrawals from cash dispensers by cash card. In each case the withdrawal (or series of withdrawals) was disputed; some writers claim – often with great indignation – that their cards could not have been used at a particular time or place to make the withdrawal because no-one else had the PIN number *[sic]*, they were many miles away from the machine concerned, and so on. Other letters described incidents in which cash dispensers had paid out money to children who had been 'playing around' or, in one dramatic case, paid out spontaneously to no-one at all! The response of the banks had generally been to deny that such things could happen, and to refer complainants to the police.'

To the best of my knowledge no bank has ever been involved in court proceedings brought against it by a customer who has claimed that his account has been debited in respect of ATM transactions which the customer did not (and allegedly could not) have made. One reason for this may be that the amounts involved have been comparatively trivial and no bank customer has felt it worthwhile to pursue his claim. Equally, banks may well have chosen to settle, for the same reason, on an *ex gratia* basis. Anecdotal evidence suggests that in a number of cases mentioned by Mr Robert Head these various 'robotic thefts' might not have been quite so straightforward as might superficially seem to be the case and that it has transpired that a member of the cardholder's household might have known more about the incident (including details of the PIN) than was originally recognised by the complainant.

Nevertheless, this is a problem that will not merely not go away but is likely to be intensified in the context of the EFTPOS system, where a third party – the retailer – will be involved in a transaction. The US Electronic Funds Transfer Act of 1978 contains detailed procedures in sections 908 and 909 aimed at resolving this kind of dispute, with specific provisions about the burden of proof, but there is nothing in that Act that answers the practical question of how in the absence of paper or signature the parties can actually resolve the 'Yes, you did: No, I didn't' issue.

The Director General of Fair Trading (in his Report on Micro-Electronics and Retailing, September 1982) has suggested that if unauthorised debits are made by EFT the card-issuing companies should set the same limit of liability (£30) on the card-holder as applies to credit cards under the Consumer Credit Act. That suggestion, however, may be regarded as an over-simplification on the grounds that it does not compare like with like. Sections 83 and 84 of the Consumer Credit Act 1974, which limit cardholders' liability for misuse of a credit card, do not touch on the matter of the card-holders' negligence, and the question that can fairly be asked is why a bank should bear any loss at all in those cases where the card-holder with a short memory has written his PIN on the card itself. By doing this, the cardholder is arguably in the same position as somebody who has signed in blank all his cheques in a new chequebook; in which case the bank would be entitled to debit his account (in the absence of timely 'stop' instructions) if those blank cheques fell into the hands of an evilly-disposed opportunist. So also, it can be argued, the customer who has written his PIN on his card acted in precisely the same way and that, in those circumstances, the whole loss should fall on the customer.

But once again this argument will ultimately depend on the question of proof. Apart from the possibility of a chance recovery of the card, how can a bank prove that a customer has been so rash as to write his PIN on the back? One is left wondering whether the PIN system is necessarily the best that can be devised. Sir Gordon Borrie, in expressing his own doubts on this point has tentatively suggested that signature or voice recognition systems may be the answer, but until some such radical change has been introduced the question of proving or disproving the use of an ATM or EFTPOS card is one that is likely to continue to be a matter of concern both to banks and their customers.

At this stage it seems appropriate to move on to more down-to-earth issues, and raise the following points, which deal with matters of proof rather than of evidence:

- The most common dispute in ATM transactions arises when the card-holder claims that his account has been wrongly debited and that he didn't make the withdrawal himself.
- I take it that no bank has allowed such a case to go to court, realising that there can be no way, if the customer continues to assert that he never used the ATM and had never disclosed his PIN to anyone, in which a bank can prove that it was entitled to debit the account with the amount shown on the ATM record.
- This kind of problem will be exacerbated when/if an EFTPOS system is introduced.

APPENDIX

Civil Evidence Act 1968

'5.(1) In any civil proceedings a statement contained in a document produced by a computer shall, subject to rules of court, be admissible as evidence of any fact stated therein of which direct oral evidence would be admissible, if it is shown that the conditions mentioned in subsection (2) below are satisfied in relation to the statement and computer in question.

(2) The said conditions are:
(a) that the document containing the statement was produced by the computer during a period over which the computer was used regularly to store or process information for the purposes of any activities regularly carried on over that period, whether for profit or not, by any body, whether corporate or not, or by any individual;
(b) that over that period there was regularly supplied to the computer in the ordinary course of those activities information of the kind contained in the statement or of the kind from which the information so contained is derived;
(c) that throughout the material part of that period the computer was operating properly or, if not, that any respect in which it was not operating properly or was out of operation during that part of that period was not such as to affect the production of the document or the accuracy of its contents; and
(d) that the information contained in the statement reproduces or is derived from information supplied to the computer in the ordinary course of those activities.

(3) Where over a period the function of storing or processing information for the purposes of any activities regularly carried on over that period as mentioned in subsection (2) (a) above was regularly performed by computers, whether:
(a) by a combination of computers operating over that period; or
(b) by different computers operating in succession over that period; or
(c) by different combinations of computers operating in succession over that period; or
(d) in any other manner involving the successive operation over that period, in whatever order, of one or more computers and one or more combinations of computers,

all the computers used for that purpose during that period shall be treated for the purposes of this Part of this Act as constituting a single computer; and references in this Part of this Act to a computer shall be construed accordingly.

(4) In any civil proceedings where it is desired to give a statement in evidence by virtue of this section, a certificate doing any of the following things, that is to say:
(a) identifying the document containing the statement and describing the manner in which it was produced;
(b) giving such particulars of any device involved in the production of that document as may be appropriate for the purpose of showing that the document was produced by a computer;
(c) dealing with any of the matters to which the conditions mentioned in subsection (2) above relate,
and purporting to be signed by a person occupying a responsible position in relation to the operation of the relevant device or the management of the relevant activities (whichever is appropriate) shall be evidence of any matter stated in the certificate; and for the purposes of this subsection it shall be sufficient for a matter to be stated to the best of the knowledge and belief of the person stating it.

(5) For the purposes of this Part of this Act:
(a) information shall be taken to be supplied to a computer if it is supplied thereto in any appropriate form and whether it is so supplied directly or (with or without human intervention) by means of any appropriate equipment;
(b) where, in the course of activities carried on by an individual or body, information is supplied with a view to its being stored or processed for the purposes of those activities by a computer operated otherwise than in the course of those activities, that information, if duly supplied to that customer, shall be taken to be supplied to it in the course of those activities;
(c) a document shall be taken to have been produced by a computer whether it was produced by it directly or (with or without human intervention) by means of any appropriate equipment.

(6) Subject to subsection (3) above, in this Part of the Act 'computer' means any device for storing and processing information, and any reference to information being derived from other information is a reference to its being derived therefrom by calculation, comparison and any other process.

Order 38, Rule 24
The procedure required under the Civil Evidence Act is contained in its own Rule of Court, namely Order 38, rule 24, the terms of which are as follows:

'24.(1) If the statement is contained in a document produced by a computer and is admissible by virtue of section 5 of the Act, the notice must have annexed to it a copy or transcript of the document containing the statement, or of the relevant part thereof, and must contain particulars of:
(a) a person who occupied a responsible position in relation to the management of the relevant activities for the purpose of which the computer was used regularly during the material period to store or process information;
(b) a person who at the material time occupied such a position in relation to the supply of information to the computer, being information which is reproduced in the statement or information from which the information contained in the statement is derived;
(c) a person who occupied such a position in relation to the operation of the computer during the material period;
and where there are two or more persons who fall within any of the foregoing subparagraphs and some only of those persons are at the date of service of the notice capable of being called as witnesses at the trial or hearing, the person particulars of whom are to be contained in the notice must be such one of those persons as is at that date so capable.

(2) The notice must also state whether the computer was operating properly throughout the material period and, if not, whether any respect on which it was not operating properly or was out of operation during any part of that period was such as to affect the production of the document in which the statement is contained or the accuracy of its contents.

(3) If the party giving the notice alleges that any person, particulars of whom are contained in the notice, cannot or should not be called as a witness at the trial or hearing for any of the reasons specified in rule 25, the notice must contain a statement to that effect specifying the reason relied on.'

To assist in practice there are guidance notes to that rule, in the following terms:

'Under para (1) of r.24, there should generally be no need to specify more than one person falling within each of the categories of persons set out in subparas (a), (b) and (c) and indeed, in many instances, it may well be that only a single person who comes within all these three categories, would need to be specified. The need for the three categories mentioned in these three subparagraphs is to provide an opportunity to the opposite party, by serving a counter-notice under r.26 to require the person named in each category to be called as a witness at the trial, so as to hear him give his evidence and if necessary to cross-examine him on the computer system, so far as it relates to the "business side" (see subpara (a)), the system of ensuring that the relevant information is accurately fed into the computer (see subpara (b)) and the 'hardware' and programming of the computer (see subpara (c)). It should be emphasised that the rule requires that the persons who are specified in the r.21 notice under these three subparagraphs should be persons who are capable of being called as witnesses at the trial rather than those who are otherwise unavailable, although they may also possess the necessary qualifications to come within these categories.

Para (2) of r.24 reflects s.5(2)(c) of the Act. This provision requires the r.21 notice relating to a statement produced by computer to state in relation to that statement that the computer had worked properly or that its failures were irrelevant to the accuracy of the statement. This provision is necessary in order to enable the opposite party to decide whether or not to dispute that the conditions specified in s.5(2)(c) of the Act had been satisfied.

Since a computer is a device by means of which information is stored or processed, a printout which is part of that device is a statement produced by the computer, and if the conditions specified in the Civil Evidence Act 1968, s.5 and r.24 are complied with, and it is clear that the operator who fed the information into the computer could not reasonably be expected to have any recollection of that information, the printout will be admitted in evidence (see *R v Ewing*,[7] decided under the Criminal Evidence Act 1965, s.1).'

7. [1983] QB 1039.

FRAUD, ERROR AND SYSTEM MALFUNCTION
A Banker's Viewpoint

Jonathan Lass

Introduction

It is no surprise that the information revolution and the technological revolution are having a profound impact on the international banking system. The huge expansion in automated computer processing coupled with significant continuous investment in banking operations is giving rise to a variety of new ways for the delivery of financial services and the speed at which information and transactions can be provided and effected.

We are seeing at the same time a significant shift from paper-based transfers of funds to those achieved by electronic means and the growth in importance of transfer systems and intermediaries. Different relationships arise, some directly involving the bank's customers but more often than not, without the knowledge of the customer. In a vast majority of cases the decision as to how to implement a customer's instruction is left entirely to banks. The customer is not involved in the mechanics of the process whereby funds are transferred – unless it goes wrong.

The rapidly changing role of communications in the banking environment, as in many other businesses, further emphasises the changing world picture. We are seeing the impact of telecommunications, and deregulation in the US and now in other parts of the world, including the UK. Telecommunications via private lines, and Value Added Networks are becoming an integral part of the banks operating environment. This though raises questions as to liability in the event of error, delay, or fraud.

The pressures on the banking system are such that we will see a massive expansion of automated systems if banks are to continue to provide basic financial services over the next decade. In the UK the number of adults with bank accounts has grown from 25 per cent to 60 per cent in the past fifteen years. It is estimated that 2,500 million cheques and 500 million credit transfers were made in 1984. Paper-based systems are slow, labour-intensive and correspondingly expensive to provide and maintain. Hence the growth in EFT systems explained elsewhere. Some are interbank such as SWIFT and CHIPS; some can link customers directly such as the new sterling system for larger value items, CHAPS. The consumer is being encouraged to use automated teller machines and cash dispensers wherever possible, and the demise of the bricks and mortar of national branch banking networks for the provision of many routine banking functions is actively being forecast by planners and strategists looking out over the next decade.

It is important to maintain a balanced view of current developments. Lawyers are remunerated by clients to provide this from time to time. In looking at the fundamentals of EFT and its implications from a legal perspective, it is possible to be swept away in a tide of technological euphoria. In reality the basic difference between our current and future environment is, I submit, one of communication. Banks have been dealing with customers for centuries and used modes of communication then available; word of mouth, writing, post, telegram, telephone, (tested) telex and now computer terminal. Because perhaps of greater unfamiliarity, there is more concentration on legal analysis of rights, obligations, duties and liabilities in relation to the new than the old.

This is partly because people were comfortable with existing processes and there was no need for the law to involve itself in a proactive manner. No one asked 'should we sue the Royal Mail' if the money transfer was delayed through the post; even if at that time such a thing were legally possible. However, with the spread of communication links and data bases, together with problems relating to access and reliability, integrity rightly raises certain concerns, which should involve the legal profession. Lawyers need to keep this change in the operating environment in mind, when we consider the issues facing banks both today and on to the next century.

We have already benefited from an operational overview of EFT systems and an examination of a number of the legal issues arising involving finality and revocability of payment, settlement systems, truncation and evidence. Also we are examining to what extent, where and in what way liability should reside and/or be excluded by banks, intermediaries and customers. Specific focus is directed to the Unfair Contract Terms Act 1977 and the Supply of Goods and Services Act 1982.

Professor Pennington has analysed in detail the question of fraud in relation to transfers involving CHAPS in the UK. My task is to look at the issues of fraud, error and systems and security in other areas as they affect banks, third parties involved in the EFT process and, of course, customers.

Definition of EFT

UNCITRAL[1] in its detailed and continuing analysis of legal

1. Draft legal guide on Electronic Funds Transfer – United Nations Commission on International Trade Law 1984–85.

issues defines EFT as 'a funds transfer in which one or more steps in the process that were previously done by paper-based techniques are now being done by electronic techniques.' The payment instruction or a significant part of the process is made in electronic form. The use of electronic impulses results in increased speed and volume and the corresponding benefit should be reduced cost for the bank customer. Interbank transfers and the maintenance of records of accounts and transactions on a computer data base are key elements of EFT. Apart from the growth of consumer 'home-banking', however, a significant proportion of EFT transactions will continue for the immediate future to have a paper-based *original* instruction.

Fraud

UNCITRAL defines this in relation to EFT as 'an unauthorised instruction, alteration of the account to which an entry is to be made or alteration of the amount of the entry'.

There are a number of possibilities:

Customers' employees

In many instances the basis is the same as in paper-based systems. Common examples would include:
- Altering payroll or vouchers process so that an authorised individual pays self or accomplice who is not so entitled.
- Deception by discovering how to access and activate the computer system, entering appropriate codes and instructions, thereby causing funds to be paid away.

Both frauds are complete when the funds are appropriated by a dishonest employee or accomplice.

There is an analogy from a legal standpoint between the above and the dishonest employee obtaining access to mechanical cheque-signing equipment or, alternatively, tested telex codes. The problems in these situations will turn on burden of proof and ability to establish the evidence, and the practical solution may fall back on relevant insurance cover (see also Security[2]).

Terminal-to-terminal link

This would apply both in a consumer context with the customer being issued with a plastic card together with Personal Identification Number and in a corporate context with passwords and

---

2. p.65 *post.*

customer identification numbers.

There are a variety of different mechanisms and techniques for providing access. In addition, bank systems have to permit differing levels of authority in respect of transactions and customers. This can be important in minimising the financial consequences of fraud, especially in consumer business.

There is a different level of security required in relation to ATMs and CDs compared with terminal links in the corporate customer's premises. Here there are problems of access and it is essential for customers to develop adequate internal control procedures. Banks devote a significant amount of resources to minimise the technical, operational risks in the systems they develop. By the same token, there is a corresponding obligation on the customer – consumer and corporate – to safeguard PINs, passwords and IDs and keep them confidential. This is a combined effort in the interests of all.

Bank employees

This includes employees gaining access to the system and entering fraudulent transfers or alternatively changing software leading to fraud *vis-à-vis* the customer or the bank.

Banks are particularly vigilant in developing and testing systems that make the potential for fraud, from whatever source, increasingly difficult. The operational sophistication, use of audit trail, internal EDP audit teams and the growing involvement of specialist accounting forms should ensure that banks providing electronic banking services are adhering to their implicit obligations to provide systems that meet prudent standards of security and reliability.

Communications interference

Growing attention is rightly being focussed on the vulnerability of the communication lines over which EFT messages are sent.

If messages can be intercepted and changed the scope for fraud would be substantial. Parallel procedures utilised by banks for encryption and authentication of message traffic are among the technical solutions adopted. Banks have to be sensitive to any threat to existing security measures. The use of logs of all funds transfer messages can provide means of verifying receipt and despatch of messages and enhance the possibility of preventing or at least being able to trace fraudulent instructions. This is clearly an area where co-operation between financial institutions, international bodies and/or governments is appropriate.

Liability for unauthorised transactions

I now turn to the results of these unfortunate events in terms of liability or 'picking up the pieces'.

Implicit here is the conduct of the customer and to what extent there can be said to be contributory negligence or imprudent conduct. Has there been a departure from reasonable and/or recommended bank procedures? Should there be different standards for consumer and corporate customers?

In agreements with corporate customers, emphasis is placed on security *re* passwords and ID's. There is a procedure where passwords are provided to each authorised employee of the customer. These can be changed at will and are accompanied by specific recommendations that they should be altered at least weekly.

The general guideline under English law was enunciated by the House of Lords per Lord Finlay in *London Joint Stock Bank Ltd v Macmillan & Arthur*,[3] 'if a (customer) draws a cheque in a manner which facilitates fraud he is guilty of a breach of duty as between himself and the banker and he will be responsible to the banker for any loss sustained by the banker as a natural and direct consequence of this breach of duty'.

In England, under the Consumer Credit Act 1974 s.84(1), a customer is liable for any unauthorised use of a credit card or lost PIN up to the first £30 or the credit limit, if lower.

Section 909 of the US Electronic Funds Transfer Act 1978 provides that a consumer is liable for an unauthorised EFT only if the card or other access is used with the PIN or equivalent. The loss is limited to $50 where report is made to the bank within two days of loss of card or unauthorised EFT or $500 if the loss is reported between two and sixty days after such event.

The only decided case to date involves an institution with which I am not wholly unfamiliar: the case; a consumer one, namely – *Ognibene v Citibank*.[4] In this case the judge held that the bank was negligent in not warning consumer customers that they should not lend their cards to third-party 'criminals' who by watching them enter their PIN could then activate the system. In this case the con-man asked to borrow Mr Ognibene's plastic card on the pretext that he was following a request from the bank service centre to test the system. Having already memorised the plaintiff's PIN, the thief withdrew $400 from Mr Ognibene's

---

3. [1918] AC 777.
4. NA 446 NYS 2d 845.

account, and then returned the card to him. The Court was influenced by the fact that there had been a few similar such cases previously, thereby giving rise to a 'notional' duty on the part of the bank to warn its customers.

The placing of the burden of proof can decide who will bear the loss as it is difficult to prove that the fraud was actually facilitated by the bank or customer as the case may be.

Errors

The UNCITRAL draft legal guide suggests four principal heads in respect of errors arising, which are specifically related to EFT. These are: (1) non-standardisation of message formats between the various EFT systems resulting in re-keying of messages; (2) re-creation of messages; (3) non-standardised procedures particularly in relation to international transfers; (4) equipment failure or software error.

Clearly in EFT there is, by definition, reliance on a wide variety of functions and equipment which involves third party providers and manufacturers. Thus a money transfer of US Dollars from a UK importer to a Japanese exporter would involve on the UK importer's side – say its UK Clearing Bank, its New York correspondent, SWIFT and CHIPS.

On the Japanese exporter's side – say its local Japanese bank, its New York correspondent to receive funds in its New York account and the same other intermediaries, carriers and networks. Computer hardware of banks, carriers, message switching and interbank money transmission services (SWIFT) and clearing house (CHIPS) with their related systems, personnel, and software are all involved.

Defects in hardware or software are potentially more serious than one individual operational mishap. Apart from specific liability, to the extent that the problem is within the control of individual institutions, then it is a question of applying resources to deal with the matter. In some circumstances greater harmonization of standards and formats would be of assistance. There are initiatives being co-ordinated under the auspices of the Banking Committee of the International Standards Organisation (ISO) and these will have a positive impact in promoting a more secure international as well as domestic operating environment.

Liability for error

This can be analysed under the following heads:

Bank statements

Under English law a customer is under no implied duty to inspect statements of account.[5] Of course, in practical terms this is one of the simplest and most direct methods of ascertaining error, fraud or discrepancies.

The US Uniform Commercial Code requires customers to exercise reasonable care and promptness in examining statements. The US Electronic Funds Transfer Act 1978 obliges banks to investigate errors, provided the financial institution is notified within 60 days of the bank statement.

Originating bank

This is based on the proposition that a bank undertakes to provide a service and the mechanics and various intermediaries involved are not determined or selected by the customer. Accordingly, in the event of error, it is the originating bank that is the best place to determine who should bear responsibility, and in the meantime its customer should be held blameless.

Breakdown in systems, computer hardware/software

In the case of the banker/customer relationship this would be governed by established contractual terms or specific express terms in respect of corporate customers or consumer customers. Banks in the UK seek to limit liability to those areas within their reasonable control taking account of the relevant tests provided in the Unfair Contract Terms Act 1977 and Supply of Goods and Services Act 1982.

As to the third party liability, ie equipment manufacturer, software house, carrier, or clearing house, we may see a greater inclination to pursue claims. This will depend on whether there is sufficient proximity between the parties and if there is reasonably foreseeable loss which can include consequential loss where there is established negligence.[6]

In this context it should be noted that the US Court of Appeals rejected a claim for *consequential* loss arising out of delay by a correspondent bank (where there was no direct contractual relationship) in processing a funds transfer resulting in cancellation of the

---

5. *Chatterton v London & County Banking Co Ltd, (1891), The Miller*, 3rd Nov., 394.
6. *Junior Books Ltd v The Veitchi Co Ltd* 1982 3 WLR 477.

proverbial charterparty.[7] The court applied the reasonable foreseeability tests enunciated in *Hadley v Baxendale*.[8]

Many of the clearing houses such as CHIPS and CHAPS, and payment instruction services such as SWIFT, have detailed rules and provisions as to liability for loss, binding on participants as terms and conditions of use and membership.

Again in the consumer area, the US Electronic Funds Transfer Act sets out a number of specific exemptions permitting a bank to refuse to make a transfer. The specific grounds are:

1. that there are insufficient funds in the consumer's account;
2. that the account is subject to legal process or other encumbrance restricting transfer;
3. that such transfer would exceed an established credit limit; or
4. that an electronic terminal has insufficient cash to complete the transaction.

There are also specific exemptions where the bank can show on a balance of probabilities that the failure was due to:

1. An act of God or other circumstances beyond its control and that it exercised reasonable care to prevent such occurrence!
2. There was a technical malfunction known to the consumer at the time of attempted transfer.

Confidentiality and security

These are fundamental elements of the banking systems and are areas in which banks have hopefully assisted in setting standards relevant to business as a whole.

Confidentiality

This is the basis of banker/customer relationship and the guiding principles were laid down in the leading case of *Tournier v National Provincial and Union Bank of England*.[9] Confidentiality of customers' data and affairs is an integral part of how banks have operated for decades and banks have detailed internal procedures to maintain and ensure confidentiality.

---

7. *Evra Corporation v Swiss Bank Corporation* [1982] 673F 2d 951.
8. (1854) 9 Ex 341.
9. [1924] 1 KB 461.

Security

The same awareness and control has to be exercised as far as practicable when third parties are brought in to assist in developing banking products and making services available to customers. An increasingly important area for banks is their use of consultants in the EDP and systems design area. This applies to software designers, carriers, and all the other parties involved in the EFT process. Strict checks and procedures have to be in place to maintain security and the highest possible standards in banks' operations.

Banks should recommend basic procedures to be in place within the customer's operations to enhance security standards and safeguards. These cover, *inter alia*, management responsibilities such as access, operating environment, input, authorisation, processing, output, audit trail, recovery and staff training. In addition to this is user control which includes passwords and security profiles. These apply more directly to corporate customers and are part of a joint process designed to benefit, enhance and protect the banker/customer relationship.

Conclusion

This analysis, as is often the case with a topic such as EFT, leaves as many questions unanswered as solved. This is to be expected, as what we are exploring are the issues and challenges posed by technological change in commerce, particularly the banking community. Issues of fraud, error, security and corresponding liability in respect thereof inevitably raise fundamental and delicate matters. These spill over into the public policy area as well in determining the correct balance between competition and co-operation.

The law in relation to many aspects cannot be regarded as fixed – understandably, because we have a paucity of jurisprudence. Some may take this to be a positive matter.

It is true that in maintaining a proper perspective only an infinitesimal number of transactions involving EFT ever reach the courts. This should not however support the argument that ongoing legal analysis of the issues, especially the more complex ones relating to liability, is otiose. On the contrary, the division of responsibilities and interaction of an increasing number of EFT participants with separate yet often overlapping relationships make the legal view more rather than less important.

Whether we like it or not, EFT is the future of much of the

banking business which it is changing more than many of us realise, whether as bankers or customers. At the same time it is providing and will continue to provide a fruitful area for analysis, debate, and creativity for the legal profession. It is up to us to meet these challenges.

FRAUD, ERROR AND SYSTEM MALFUNCTION
A Lawyer's Viewpoint

Robert Pennington

In dealing with the legal distribution of the burden of losses resulting from fraud, errors and malfunctioning of equipment in connection with electronic fund transfers, a primary distinction must be made between the position of the ordinary bank customer who uses the facilities of CHAPS for making and receiving payments simply as an alternative to the credit transfer system, and the position of a settlement bank customer which is either a bank or financial institution participating in CHAPS or a commercial or industrial concern which is linked to CHAPS by computer. The rights and liabilities of the former kind of customer will be regulated by much the same rules as govern his position as a customer who makes and receives payments by cheques, credit transfers and bankers' orders, and it is unlikely that payments made by or to him will call for special contractual terms beyond those which are expressed or implied in his contract with the bank as its customer. The non-settlement bank participant and the commercial customer connected to CHAPS by computer will have an active role to play in operating the system, and because it may expose the settlement bank it employs to liability to other settlement banks and their customers, its legal relationship with its own settlement bank will be regulated by a special express contract supplementing its general contract with that bank.

It is proposed therefore to examine successively the legal rights and liabilities of the ordinary customer of a settlement bank who instructs it to make occasional payments through CHAPS, and those of the non-settlement bank participant and the customer connected by computer with CHAPS through the mediation of a settlement bank.

The CHAPS mandate

An instruction for a CHAPS payment given to a settlement bank will presumably resemble the instruction form which is currently used by solicitors to make same-day payments on the completion of property transactions, and will contain the same essential information as a credit transfer instruction, namely, the name of the payer and payee, their respective banks and branches, their respective account numbers and the amount to be transferred. The instruction will be the mandate of the payer's bank to make the payment, and if the bank makes the payment through CHAPS before the mandate has been effectively revoked and without departing in any degree from the instruction, the bank will have discharged its mandate, will incur no liability to anyone and will be entitled to debit its customer's account with the payment made plus the notified charge for its services. Although CHAPS is advertised as providing a facility for payment to the payee on the same day as the payment instruction is given to the paying bank, I think it unlikely that the court would imply a guarantee of payment on that day by the paying bank. Settlement banks protect themselves against instructions notified within an hour before CHAPS transactions close at 3.00 pm not being processed on the same day, but even if an instruction were notified before 2.00 pm, the obligation of the paying bank is simply to act as expeditiously as possible in the circumstances[1] and if payment on the same day were prevented by a mechanical breakdown, pressure of work arising from instructions previously received, or a defect or default on the receiving bank's side of the gateway, the paying bank would not be liable to its customer for the delay.

Vitiating factors

The problems which arise when the customer's instruction to transfer funds is itself affected by a legally recognised defect can be solved by the rules which have already been established in connection with cheques and payment orders on which paying banks have acted. If the customer's instructions are ambiguous (eg, as to the identity of a payee company which is a member of a group of companies with similar names, or as to which of several accounts held by the same payee the transfer should be made), the bank is protected if it carries out the instructions in good faith and upon a reasonable interpretation of the customer's intentions.[2] The fact that the transaction between the customer and the payee which gives rise to the customer's instructions to the bank is itself vitiated by fraud or misrepresentation practised by the payee on the customer, or by mistake as to the validity or the

---

1. *Hare v Henty* (1861) 10 CBNS 66.
2. *Pettman v Keble* (1805) 9 CB 701; *Broom v Hall* (1859) 7 CBNS 503; *Westminster Bank Ltd v Hilton* (1926) 43 TLR 124.

factual basis for that transaction on the part of the customer (eg, mistake as to the identity of the payee or the existence of the subject matter of the transaction), does not affect the validity of the instructions to the bank, and it is protected if it carries out the customer's instructions to make payment to the payee's bank without knowledge of the vitiating factor.

Fraud, misrepresentation and mistake
Any fraud or misrepresentation entitling the customer to avoid the underlying transaction does not invalidate it completely, but merely entitles the customer to rescind it and to seek restitution of any amount paid to the payee. Consequently, third parties (including the customer's bank) are entitled to treat the transaction as valid and effectual and also to treat derivative transactions (including instructions to make payments under the main transaction) as legally effectual until the main transaction is rescinded, and even then if they acted in good faith without knowledge or suspicion of the fraud or misrepresentation, they cannot be prejudicially affected retrospectively by the rescission.[3] The effect of mistake by a customer as to a fundamental matter affecting the main transaction may have a somewhat different effect, because if sufficiently serious it may make that transaction void at common law, even though the total invalidity of the transaction may result in third parties who have acted in good faith losing rights which they have acquired and incurring liabilities.[4] However, a mistake which invalidates a main transaction does not necessarily avoid derivative or consequential transactions; this is so if the derivative transaction, taken in isolation, would not itself be avoided by one of the parties making a mistake of the kind which invalidates the main transaction. The courts have referred to such mistakes as 'collateral', or mistakes made between different parties, and have upheld the derivative transaction at the instance of the party to it who neither made the mistake or knew that a mistake had been made.[5] In the context of a payment made by a bank on instructions from its customer, this means that the fact that the transaction under which the payment is made is void because of the customer's mistake does not invali-

---

3. *White v Gordon* (1851) 10 CB 919; *Babcock v Lawson* (1879) 4 QBD 394.
4. *Hardman v Booth* (1853) 1 H & C 803; *Cundy v Lindsay* (1878) 3 App Cas 459.
5. *Aiken v Short* (1856) 1 H & N 210.

date the instructions to the bank to make payment or the payment itself when made.[6]

Unauthorised payment
The one factor which will invalidate instructions to a bank to make a payment is that the customer whose account is debited did not authorise the payment. In the case of a payment through CHAPS this means either that the signatory of the written instruction form forged the customer's signature (an occurrence which is likely to be infrequent if the bank requires instructions to be signed on the bank's premises, or at least to be delivered there personally by the customer), or that the signatory signed the instruction form with his own signature on behalf of the named customer and he either had no authority to give such instructions, or he had a limited authority but exceeded it. The bank's position if it acts on the instruction is the same as if it pays a cheque bearing a forged or unauthorised signature; it acts outside its mandate in acting on the forged or unauthorised instruction and so does not make the payment on its customer's behalf and cannot debit his account.[7] If the customer has represented the signatory to be his agent invested with a wider authority to instruct the bank to make payments than the signatory has in fact been given, the customer will, of course, be estopped from claiming that the bank made a payment outside its mandate if the signatory was acting within his apparent authority when giving the instruction; and if the customer ratifies an instruction given by his agent after the payment is made, the bank may debit the customer's account even though the agent had no authority to give the instruction in the first place. Furthermore, if the customer is a company whose directors have been irregularly appointed or have continued to act as directors after their period of office has expired, the bank is protected in effecting payment instructions which the directors give, purporting to act on the company's behalf, and this is so even if the formal mandate given by the company is itself signed on the company's behalf by such *de facto* directors.[8] Finally, if the bank cannot rely on a mandate given by its customer because the giving of the payment instruction is outside the actual and apparent authority of the signatory, the bank may still debit its

6. *Chambers v Miller* (1862) 13 CBNS 125; *Pollard v Bank of England* (1871) LR 6 QB 623; *Deutsche Bank v Beriro & Co* (1895) 73 LT 669.
7. *Orr v Union Bank* (1854) 1 Macq H L 315; *Catlin v Cyprus Finance Corpn (London) Ltd* [1983] QB 759.
8. *Mahony v East Holyford Mining Co* (1875) LR 7 HL 869.

customer's account to the extent that the payment has discharged an enforceable liability of the customer; this is because the bank is subrogated to the rights of the customer's creditor who has been paid, and is entitled to set off the debt which the customer owed him against the credit balance of the customer's account.[9]

Forgery
The modifications made by case law to the rule that a bank may not debit its customer's account with a payment made by it on the instructions of an agent acting outside his authority, are not paralleled by similar modifications when the payment is made under a forged instruction. It is doubtful whether a forged signature can be ratified by the person whose signature it purports to be, despite the opinion of Lord Blackburn in *M'Kenzie v British Linen Co*[10] that ratification, in the sense of an assertion by that person that he will treat the signature as though it had been given with his prior authorisation, does make any obligation created by the forged instrument binding on him. The directly contrary view was taken by the court in *Brook v Hook*[11] where it was held that ratification as distinct from an assertion that the signature was genuine, could only amount to a gratuitous promise by the person whose signature had been forged to fulfil the obligation created by the forged document although it was not binding on him, and such a promise was ineffective for lack of consideration. On the other hand, a positive assertion by that person that the forged signature was his own would estop him from repudiating liability to the person to whom the assertion was made and who relied on it to his detriment, though such an assertion in respect of one of a series of forged documents would not necessarily estop him from repudiating liability on the others.[12]

Estoppel
Nevertheless, failure by a customer of a bank to respond to enquiries by it as to the genuineness of several cheques drawn on his account, or several instructions for payments out of his account, may estop the customer from later contending that the signatures on those and later similar instruments are forgeries.[13]

9. *Liggett (Liverpool) Ltd v Barclays Bank Ltd* [1928] 1 KB 46; *London Intercontinental Trust Ltd v Barclays Bank Ltd* [1980] 1 Lloyd's Rep 241.
10. *M'Kenzie v British Linen Co* (1881) 6 App Cas 82, 99.
11. *Brook v Hook* (1871) LR 6 Ex 89.
12. *Morris v Bethall* (1869) LR 5 CP 47.
13. *Brown v Westminster Bank Ltd* [1964] 2 Lloyd's Rep 187.

The fact that a customer has made it possible for cheques or payment instructions to be forged (for example, by the directors of a company leaving cheque or payment instruction forms in the custody of the company's secretary, who completes them without the authorisation of the directors and forges directors' signatures on them), does not make the customer responsible for the forgeries, and this is so even if the forgeries could be detected by the customer checking statements of account periodically sent to him by his bank.[14] It is uncertain what degree of carelessness on the part of a customer must be shown in providing for the safe custody of cheques, payment instruction forms and facsimile signature stamps and in failing to verify statements of account which show net balances at startling variance from what would normally be expected, in order that the bank may pass the burden of loss resulting from forgeries to him. From the present state of judicial authority it would seem that this can be done only if he knowingly tolerates or actively conspires in the forgery of his signature on cheques or payment instructions, or if he asserts the genuineness of the documents when he is questioned by the bank or does not reply to its questions.

The duties of collecting and paying banks

Payment through CHAPS

When a customer has instructed his bank to make a payment through CHAPS, the remaining steps to effect payment are taken by the bank in co-operation with the payee's bank. It is therefore tempting to treat the operation as being wholly at the risk of the paying bank, so that if payment is made incorrectly or is not made at all, the resulting loss falls wholly on the paying bank, including loss suffered by the customer because the transaction in connection with which the payment instruction was given is terminated or repudiated by the other party. It is easy to make such an assumption from the common law rules governing the liabilities of banks in respect of the payment and collection of cheques. Their liabilities at common law in that context appear to be absolute, because both paying and collecting banks are liable absolutely at common law for the conversion of a cheque if they pay or collect it on behalf of a person who has no title to it,

---

14. *Kepitagalla Rubber Estates Ltd v National Bank of India* [1909] 2 KB 1010; *London Joint Stock Bank Ltd v Macmillan* [1918] AC 777; *Tai Hingh Cotton Mill Ltd v Liu Chong Hing Bank Ltd* [1985] 2 All ER 947.

and it is only because of the intervention of statute that the liability has been reduced to one for negligence. In other respects the liabilities of paying and collecting banks in connection with the presentation and payment of cheques are not absolute, however; an examination of the steps in the cheque clearing shows that the legal status of the banks changes as the various steps are carried out, and the nature and extent of their duties accordingly.

The collection and payment of cheques
A bank which receives a cheque for collection is a bailee of it and an agent of its customer to effect presentation and collect the amount of the cheque. At this stage the collecting bank's duty to its customer is simply to exercise reasonable care, but it cannot diminish that duty by employing another bank as a sub-agent and delegating its functions, and if it does this it is vicariously liable for the negligence of the other bank as though it were its own.[15] Whether a sub-agent bank is employed or not, the collecting bank escapes liability if it shows that all proper care was taken to collect the amount of the cheque, and that the failure to collect was not the result of its acts or omissions.[16] Consequently, if a cheque is fortuitously lost in transit, or if its presentation is fortuitously delayed until after the drawer or his bank has become insolvent, the collecting bank is not liable to its customer. Once the cheque has been paid to the collecting bank or its sub-agent, however, the collecting bank's liability to its customer becomes absolute, and he can recover the amount of the cheque by suing the collecting bank in debt.[17] This is because of the legal relationship of the bank and its customer in respect of the amount which has or should be credited to his account; that relationship is not that of agent and principal, but debtor and creditor.[18] Consequently, if the collecting bank employs another bank to collect a cheque and the amount of the cheque is paid to the other bank but it fails to account to the collecting bank for that amount, the collecting bank is absolutely liable to its customer for the amount of the cheque. A paying bank is under a corresponding duty of care to its customer, the drawer of the cheque, and it cannot debit his account with the amount of the cheque if it should have realised that its content or presentation were irregular.[19] In one respect a

15. *Calico Printers' Association v Barclays Bank Ltd* (1930) 36 Com Cas 71.
16. *Mackersy v Ramsays Bonar and Co* (1843) 9 Cl & F 818, 845 per Lord Campbell.
17. *Mackersy v Ramsays Bonar and Co (supra); Clark v Oriental Bank Corporation* (1878) 3 App Cas 325.
18. *Foley v Hill* (1848) 2 HLC 28.
19. *Bellamy v Majoribanks* (1852) 7 Exch 389.

paying bank's liability is absolute, however. If it pays a cheque outside the limits of the mandate given to it by its customer, it cannot debit his account, even though it has not been guilty of negligence. Consequently, a paying bank cannot debit the amount of a cheque it has paid if it is a forgery,[20] or at common law (now modified by statute) if the cheque bears a forged indorsement,[21] or if it is signed by one director of the drawer company when the mandate called for two directors' signatures.[22] Finally, it is clear that a paying bank's duties to exercise care and to act within the limits of its mandate are owed only to its own customer. If it has been put in funds to pay a cheque by the drawer and it pays someone other than the holder of the cheque or a bank collecting on his behalf, the paying bank is under no liability to the holder, whether or not it can debit the amount of the cheque to its own customer's account.[23]

Obligations of the banks under CHAPS

An examination of the liabilities of paying and collecting banks in connection with cheque payments gives an insight as to the way in which the courts categorise the changing status of banks in the course of clearing operations and construct a scheme of varying liabilities accordingly, but it gives no direct lead to the way in which the courts will act when they deal with the liabilities of paying and collecting banks for losses resulting from the defective working of CHAPS. There is no real analogy between the cheque clearing and CHAPS, because most of the steps from the issue to the payment of a cheque are taken outside the banking system, whereas a CHAPS payment is effected wholly within the banking system once the initial instruction to make it has been given by the payer to the paying bank. A closer analogy to a CHAPS payment is a payment by credit transfer, and CHAPS is functionally simply a credit transfer system operated by the intercommunicating computers of the paying and collecting banks instead of by the banks interchanging credit vouchers and settling net balances between them each day. Unfortunately, however, there is no case law on liabilities arising from mishaps in the credit clearing, apart from a few cases on special credit transfers not involving the general credit clearing, and in those cases the only question in issue was to the time when payment had been made. The deduc-

20. *Orr v Union Bank* (1854) 1 Macq HL 513.
21. *Robarts v Tucker* (1851) 16 QB 560.
22. *Liggett (Liverpool) Ltd v Barclays Bank Ltd (supra)*.
23. *Auchteroni v Midland Bank Ltd* [1928] 2 KB 294.

tion of rules of common law governing liabilities from the defective operation of CHAPS must therefore start from first principles, and the case law on banks' liabilities in connection with the collection and payment of cheques will be of only incidental assistance.

Contract between banker and customer
The obligations of paying and receiving banks to their respective customers in carrying out payment operations under CHAPS will, in the absence of specially agreed terms, be the obligations arising under the general contract between bank and customer which is impliedly entered into when the bank opens an account at the customer's request. The basic obligation of the bank is to carry out its customers' instructions and to act in banking transactions in which he is involved with reasonable skill and care so as to protect his interests, and the standard of skill and care which the bank must exhibit is that of the reasonably competent banker acting in accordance with accepted current practice.[24] This duty is now subsumed under the general duty imposed by s.13 of the Supply of Goods and Services Act 1982 on persons who supply services under contract to exercise reasonable skill and care in doing so. Nevertheless, the standard of skill and care required of banks in dealing with their customers' affairs will continue to be that fixed by case law, since the statute is merely a restatement of common law rules in generalised terms. Superimposed on the bank's duty to exercise reasonable skill and care is the duty to its customer to conform to his mandate in respect of each transaction. This duty is absolute but negative in character, and it applies principally to the paying bank. The payer authorises his bank to make a payment through CHAPS only of a specified amount to a specified bank for the account of a specified payee.

If the payment message passed through the CHAPS gateway differs from the payer's instructions to his bank in respect of any of these three specified matters, the paying bank acts without the payer's mandate, and whether it or any of its employees or agents has been guilty of negligence or not, it cannot debit the amount paid to his account. This does not mean that any loss resulting from a departure from the paying bank's mandate is not retrievable and that the ultimate loss will necessarily fall on the paying bank; the payer and the paying bank can exercise the right of

---

24. *Selangor United Rubber Estates Ltd v Cradock (No 3)* [1968] 2 All ER 1073; *Karak Rubber Co Ltd v Burden (No 2)* [1972] 1 All ER 1210.

recovery and restitution mentioned below against the collecting bank and the payee, and to a limited extent, against third parties. Nevertheless, the paying bank does incur legal liability to its customer, and if the remedies of recovery and restitution prove unavailing, it will bear the loss itself.

Of course, not all mishaps in connection with payments through CHAPS will involve a disregard of the limits of the paying bank's mandate. If a payment is not made at all or is made only after a delay, the paying bank does not act outside its mandate, and will be able to escape liability for consequential loss suffered by its customer if it can show that the failure or delay was not attributable to the negligence of itself or its employees or agents.

The mandate of a collecting bank in connection with a CHAPS payment is of less importance than that of the paying bank. Most customers impliedly give an open mandate to their banks permitting all incoming items to be credited to their account. If a customer instructs his bank that a particular payment, or payments generally from a particular source, are not to be accepted and credited to his account, the bank would act outside its mandate if it accepted such a payment. In the context of CHAPS this would mean that the receiving bank would be free to acknowledge the arrival of the payment message through its gateway, but would as soon as possible have to transmit a message to the paying bank that it intends to make a return payment. This could be particularly important when the payee has instructed his bank not to accept a particular payment after a specified time so that he may exercise the right to terminate a contract with the payer (eg, to terminate a charterparty because of the charterer's failure to pay an instalment of the hire payments promptly). Technically, acceptance by the receiving bank of such a payment is a breach of its mandate for which it is absolutely liable, but it would also seem in any case to involve it in liability for negligence.

For whose acts the bank is responsible

The persons for whose acts a paying or receiving bank is legally responsible will be the same in connection with CHAPS transactions as in connection with other banking transactions. Banks are liable for the wrongful acts of their employees while acting in the course of their employment, whether the employees act negligently or deliberately. A bank will be liable, therefore, if an employee engaged to work in its EFT department makes a payment through CHAPS when he knows that the customer on whose behalf the payment purports to be made has not authorised it, and the employee's purpose is to defraud the customer.[25] Banks are also responsible for the acts and omissions of independent contractors, usually other banks, whom they engage to carry out the whole or part of transactions for which they have accepted instructions from their customers, but the responsibility of such banks is limited to acts and omissions of the independent contractors in carrying out the tasks confided to them, and does not extend to unrelated acts.[26] In general, banks are not liable for the acts of third parties who are neither employees nor independent contractors, but who use the bank's equipment or facilities without their consent or acquiescence to carry out wrongful acts which cause loss to the bank's customers. Nevertheless, banks are subject to an overriding contractual duty to their customers to take reasonable precautions to prevent unauthorised persons using bank equipment or facilities so as to cause loss to their customers, and also to take reasonable steps to minimise and recuperate such loss when third parties have acted improperly.

The duty to provide a proper security system
In the context of CHAPS, fulfilment of the settlement banks' duty of care means that they must install and operate reasonably effective security systems to prevent unauthorised persons using bank terminals to transmit or alter payment messages with the consequence that amounts are improperly debited to customer's accounts. The coding and password arrangements at present established when combined with the separation of the functions of entering, authorising and releasing payment messages and the encryption of messages transmitted, should be adequate for this purpose, but as new methods of perpetrating computer frauds emerge, it will be necessary for banks to install additional defensive devices evolved by current technology in order to satisfy their duty of care to their customers.

The one aspect of the CHAPS network which makes it vulnerable at present is the possibility of tapping into the land line which connects a CHAPS terminal with the control centre of the settlement bank through which it transmits payment messages.

25. *Barwick v English Joint Stock Bank* (1867) LR 2 Ex 259; *Lloyd v Grace, Smith & Co* [1912] AC 716.
26. *Equitable Trust Company of New York v Dawson Partners Ltd* (1926) 25 Lloyd's LILR 90.

Although the encryption should protect the integrity of payment messages properly sent from the terminal and prevent the insertion of unauthorised messages, the technology now available to organised commercial crime makes the production of small unscrambling devices and equipment for transmitting identically scrambled messages a distinct possibility in the fairly near future. The duty of care owed by settlement banks to their customers does not require them to guarantee that such devices will be made totally ineffective, but it will require banks to adopt the most effective means currently available for combating them. However, it is probable that the legal obligation of the settlement banks to do so will not be called in question for the good commercial reason that out of self-interest the banks will promote continuing research to elaborate new protective devices and procedures and install those of them which are practicable, and meanwhile will themselves bear the financial loss which results from fraudulent manipulation of the CHAPS system as part of their operating expenses.

Revocation of a payment instruction

A payment message entered on a CHAPS terminal may be abandoned or cancelled at the request of the payer if the message has gone no further than reaching the status of awaiting authorisation, release or approval. Payment is not in fact made until the payment message has been transmitted through the gateway and acknowledged by the receiving bank; until an acknowledgement by the receiving bank has been given, the payment is conditional only, because the failure of the receiving bank to give an acknowledgement by the end of the day, results in the payment automatically being cancelled. Until payment is acknowledged the receiving bank will not credit the payee, and so failure to acknowledge receipt of the payment on the day on which it is made means that same-day value will not be given. Under the general law a customer of a bank may revoke an instruction which he has given to it at any time before payment is made.[27] Because a paying bank must give effect to valid revocation instructions given by its customer, it would seem, in the absence of agreement to the contrary, that a paying bank cannot debit its customer's account with the amount of a payment if it receives a

---

27. *Morrell v Wootton* (1852) 16 Beav 197; *Mardorf Peach & Co Ltd v Attica Sea Carriers Corpn of Liberia* [1976] QB 835.

revocation instruction after it has entered, authorised and released the item for payment but before the payment message has been transmitted to the receiving bank through the gateway and acknowledged by it. To ensure that settlement banks are not put in this position, they should make it clear on their payment instruction forms that a payment instruction will become irrevocable when it has been accepted or acted on by the bank. The fact that in the CHAPS Clearing Rules, r2(b) provides that CHAPS payments must be 'irrevocable, guaranteed, unconditional sterling payments for same-day settlement' does not protect the paying bank, because the Clearing Rules are only binding contractually between settlement banks, and form no part of the contract between a settlement bank and its customers.

Recovery of payments

If a CHAPS payment has been completed and included in the daily settlement figures for transfers of net balances between the accounts kept by the settlement banks at the Bank of England, it may be possible for the payer or the paying bank to recover the amount paid from the payee or the receiving bank under the rules of common law or equity. The widest rights of recovery are those available to the payer against the payee. If the transaction between the payer and the payee is void (eg, payment made under an illegal contract where statute makes the contract illegal in order to protect persons in the payer's position), or voidable (eg, for fraud or misrepresentation), or the transaction no longer exists (eg, payment under a contract which the payee has already terminated), the payer may recover the amount he has paid by a common law action for money had and received or an equitable action for restitution. The rights of a paying bank to recover from the receiving bank or the payee are narrower, because it can rely only on a defect in the payment operation, and not one which only affects the underlying transaction between the payer and the payee. For example, a paying bank may recover a payment made by it on presentation of a forged bill of exchange or cheque,[28] or of a genuine bill or cheque which bears a forged indorsement,[29] or of a cheque which has been altered and thereby invalidated.[30] The

---

28. *Cocks v Masterman* (1829) 9 B & C 280; *National Westminster Bank Ltd v Barclays Bank International Ltd* [1975] QB 654.
29. *Wilkinson v Johnson* (1824) 3 B & C 428; *London and River Plate Bank Ltd v Bank of Liverpool Ltd* [1896] 1 QB 7.
30. *Imperial Bank of Canada v Bank of Hamilton* [1903] AC 49.

basis of the bank's claim is that it has paid the amount of the bill or cheque under a mistake of fact as to its authenticity, which is obviously an essential condition of its willingness to make payment at all.

In a recent case, however, the court has expanded the range of mistakes which may entitle the paying bank to recover, by permitting a bank to recover the amount of a cheque which it had paid by oversight after the drawer had countermanded payment.[31] The correctness of this decision is questionable, because the mistake made by the paying bank did not relate to the payment operation (ie, the relationship between the paying and receiving banks and their acts in making and receiving payment) but to the authority given by the paying bank's customer for it to make the payment and debit his account. It is certain, however, that a paying bank cannot recover payment of a cheque made under a mistake as to the sufficiency of the credit balance of the drawer's account with it.[32] A paying bank may recover a payment made under a relevant mistake of fact, either from the payee or from the receiving bank, and the receiving bank must repay despite its ignorance of the mistake at the time it received payment; however, the liability of the receiving bank is limited to the part of the amount received, which the payee has not drawn out of his account with the bank before it is notified of the paying bank's claim.[33]

The rights of a payer and paying bank to recover amounts paid by means of CHAPS will be exactly the same as their rights to recover other payments where the payment operation or the underlying transaction is defective. The substantive right of recovery is in no way affected by the method of payment employed. However, one impediment to recovery of payments under bills of exchange and cheques which the courts have imposed in certain cases will not apply to CHAPS payments. The early cases which recognised a right of recovery when a forged bill of exchange or a genuine bill bearing forged indorsements was paid in good faith, made the right of recovery conditional on the plaintiff's claim being notified to the payee or his bank within the period allowed for the holder of the bill to give notice of dishonour to prior parties; this requirement treated the exercise of

---

31. *Barclays Bank Ltd v WJ Simms Son and Cooke (Southern) Ltd* [1980] QB 677.
32. *Chambers v Miller* (1862) 1 CBNS 125.
33. *National Westminster Bank Ltd v Barclays Bank International Ltd (supra); Barclays Bank Ltd v WJ Simms Son and Cooke (Southern) Ltd (supra).*

the right of recovery as retrospective dishonour of the bill, and ensured that the holder still had time within which to preserve his rights against other parties to the bill.[34] This requirement is, of course, inapplicable when recovery is sought of a CHAPS payment, because there are no other parties to the transaction beyond the payer and payee and their respective banks, and there are no possible rights of recourse against third persons. If a bill of exchange were paid by the acceptor to the holder by means of a CHAPS payment, however, the requirement of prompt notice of the payer's claim to the payee and his bank would be necessary, not because the payment was made through CHAPS, but because of the rules governing the underlying transaction (ie, the bill of exchange). The validity of the requirement of prompt notice of reclaim has been doubted in one recent case,[35] and if it turns out to be unfounded, the period within which an action may be brought to recover a payment vitiated by mistake or other defect will be the normal one of six years from the time the payment is made, or the mistake is discovered, or should with reasonable diligence have been discovered.[36]

Direct communication by customer to CHAPS

The foregoing discussion of the law governing CHAPS payments has assumed that a written payment instruction is given by a customer to a branch of a settlement bank and the payment message is transmitted by that bank's employees through the bank's control centre and gateway to the receiving bank. The customer may have a direct connection with CHAPS, however, whether as a participant bank or financial institution with its own terminal, or as a commercial customer whose mainframe computer transmits payment instructions to CHAPS through a packet switching service unit. In that case payment instructions will be transmitted by the customer's own staff directly through the settlement bank's control centre and gateway, and the only intervention of the settlement bank will be to give its approval to payment messages so as to ensure that the individual payment and gross or net operating limits agreed with the settlement bank are adhered to.

34. *Wilkinson v Johnson (supra); Cocks v Masterman (supra).*
35. *National Westminster Bank Ltd v Barclays Bank International Ltd (supra)*), though affirmed in another (*Barclays Bank Ltd v WJ Simms Son and Cooke (Southern) Ltd (supra)*.
36. Limitation Act 1980, ss. 5, 32 (1).

The responsibility for payment instructions is therefore undertaken by the customer, and so at common law, if improper instructions are transmitted by the customer's employees, agents or other persons who have access to its terminal or computer with the customer's consent, the resulting loss will be borne by the customer, because by its conduct in giving access to the terminal or computer the customer has consented to bear the risk of loss. On the other hand, no such consent can be implied when improper payment instructions are transmitted by persons who are not employed or authorised by the customer to use the terminal, but it does not follow that the resulting loss has to be borne by the settlement bank, even though the payments are made through it and settled by it with the receiving banks. The reason for this is that the settlement bank has not acted on a mandate from its customer in making the payments, but has merely provided the facilities by which the customer has made the payments itself. The bank's duty to the customer is therefore confined to exercising reasonable skill and care in providing those facilities, and if it takes reasonable steps to ensure that the customer's terminal or computer is adequate and properly connected and that the land line connecting the terminal to CHAPS is secure from tapping, it fulfils its duty of care.

The cause of the loss when improper payment instructions are transmitted from the customer's terminal or computer is the action of third persons for whom the bank is not responsible, and the customer's redress is against them alone. To ensure that customers who have terminal and computer links to CHAPS are aware of this, settlement banks include in their contracts with such customers a term that the customer 'will assume the whole risk of fraudulent, unauthorised or otherwise improper use of (the) password facility (provided by the bank), data processing terminals and equipment and telecommunication equipment'. On the assumption that the settlement bank has checked the adequacy and security of the terminal and the link to CHAPS, such a term will be safe from challenge as an unreasonable condition in a standard form contract under the Unfair Contract Terms Act 1977, s.3, since it merely reflects the position the parties would occupy if there were no such term in the contract between them.

THE QUANTUM AND LIMITS OF LIABILITY

Eric Woods

The consequences of fraud, mistake or malfunction are usually the unjust enrichment of one and the unjust impoverishment of another. The consequences are unjust because they arise not by agreement but by the criminal intention of one party, mistake on the part of one or both parties, electronic breakdown or some other event as a result of which the electronic system does not work. The views expressed in this note must not be taken to be those of any bank with which I am associated – nor should they be regarded as my final thoughts. They are assembled to provide the basis for discussion.

Movement away from signed instruction

Six examples of malfunction
The relevant contract will usually be concluded between a bank and its customer or between two banks. I quote from the *Encyclopaedia of Banking Law*: 'The relationship between banker and customer is contractual and founded on one contract, which normally includes the relationship of creditor and debtor with regard to the balance in the customer's bank account and the relationship of principal and agent in respect of the payment of the customer's cheques drawn on the customer's bank account.' Above all it is a continuing relationship. The obligation to sign and write is giving way with advanced technology to the push-button-plastic-card system. Does such a system necessarily involve changes in the historic contractual relationship? Changes have, in fact, come gradually. From our own experience we can identify the consequences of moving from the particular handwritten and signed document, and note the protection the banker has sought against each innovation. The sequence of these kinds of changes in the banking system might well be discerned from the following:
1. mechanically signed/prepared cheques and/or lithographed cheques, typewritten cheques and printed cheques;
2. telegraphed or telexed instructions to pay or transfer funds;
3. telephoned instructions to pay, to accept deposits, or to operate within money markets;
4. cash cards and withdrawal of funds from machines;
5. direct debiting arrangements;
6. money transfer under CHAPS; and, in the future

7. EFTPOS.

Let us postulate for each of the first six methods of money transmission some kind of malfunction, for example:
- county council cheques, signed and produced by machine, multiply by one hundred times the amounts of a series of payments, which are not noticed until the council sees its bank statements;
- a telex from Singapore to pay a nephew £5,000 is misconstrued; the bank pays to the nephew's account a sum in the 'amount' of the telephone number;
- a banker receives a telephone call from a corporate treasurer; he thought the instruction was 'transfer DM 50,000' but the treasurer only intended him to transfer DM 15,000;
- a cash card holder indiscreetly allows his mistress to use his cash card to draw £50 and gives her the PIN; subsequently he finds that £500 has been withdrawn from his account;
- a direct debit arrangement is made for the payment of insurance premiums, but the insurance company fails to ask for regular payments and contends that the life policy has lapsed;
- lastly and more recently, funds are input into the CHAPS system and pass out from the gateway of the paying bank. Before the account of a receiving banker has recorded the credit, there is a total mechanical breakdown within the main computer, with the result that the debit to one account subsists without the corresponding credit to the account of the other bank.

How special terms have varied the banker/customer contract
How has the general contractual relationship between the parties been varied to facilitate these changes in money transition systems?

From the county council an indemnity will have been obtained whereby the county council indemnifies the bank against all consequences which the bank may suffer or sustain by reason of any of the 'mechanically signed or completed cheques being issued without authority, the bank being entitled to honour such cheques according to the tenor as presented and to debit the county council's account'.

Where there are telegraphed or telexed instructions, they will not be the subject of any formal contract but will be governed by arrangements, if any, made previously between the customer and the bank about intended telex/telegraphic instructions. If there are no such arrangements compliance with the instructions depends upon the bank's satisfaction with their authenticity and its willingness in such circumstances to take a risk.

The developing practice of giving telephone instructions must still be regarded as an unsatisfactory method of instructing a banker. As with the telegraphic and telex instructions it is important to establish the identity of the caller. There is also a greater possibility of misunderstanding on oral instruction.

No indemnity is normally requested by a bank for the occasional instruction. But corporate customers using money market facilities usually provide specific board resolutions authorising certain officials of the company to give oral instructions. Ideally the company should contract on the basis that the instructions, as understood by the bank, are as recorded on a memorandum by the bank subsequently given to the company.

A cash card is subject to a formal agreement incorporating an obligation by the card-holder to keep the PIN secret.

Direct debiting arrangements depend on the introduction of the debiting party to the banking system by a sponsoring bank (and include a specific indemnity in general terms for any wrongly instigated debit so that the bankers to the customer wrongly debited are indemnified against the consequences).

Under the CHAPS system there is no special agreement between banker and customer. The customer leaves the bank free to give effect to his wishes in whatever way the bank may choose, so long as prompt payment to a particular account with another bank is achieved.

Limitations and restrictions on the special terms

What limitations and restrictions apply to the special contract to govern the new services? They seem to fall into two categories. The first concerns the consequences of the doctrine, if such it is, of equality of bargaining power. The second, which has continuous and very difficult implications, concerns the consequences of the Unfair Contract Terms Act, 1977.

Equality of bargaining power
First in time, the concept of 'equality of bargaining power', developed from the readiness of the courts of equity to upset unconscionable bargains. There is an increasing need for such equality where standard forms of contract are concerned as was first judicially identified in *Esso Petroleum Limited v Harper's Garage (Stourport) Limited*.[1] Lord Pearce said: 'It is important

---

1. [1968] AC 269.

that the court, in weighing the question of reasonableness, should give full weight to commercial practices and to the generality of contracts made freely by parties bargaining on equal terms.'

The music boom of the 1970s contributed at least two decisions to further the development of the equality of bargaining powers and in *A. Schroeder Music Publishing Co Ltd v Macaulay*.[2] Lord Reid said: 'But if contractual restrictions appear to be unnecessary or to be reasonably capable of enforcement in an oppressive manner then they must be justified before they can be enforced.'

Lord Diplock expressed the following opinion:

'It is, in my view, salutary to acknowledge that in refusing to enforce provisions of a contract whereby one party agrees for the benefit of the other party to exploit or to refrain from exploiting his own earning-power, the public policy which the court is implementing is not some 19th century economic theory about the benefit to the general public of freedom of trade, but the protection of those where bargaining power is weak against being forced by those where bargaining power is stronger to enter into bargains that are unconscionable. Under the influence of Bentham and of *laissez-faire* the courts in the 19th century abandoned the practice of applying the public policy against unconscionable bargains to contracts generally, as they had formerly done to any contract considered to be usurious; but the policy survived in its application to penalty clauses and to relief against forfeiture and also to the special category of contracts in restraint of trade. If one looks at the reasoning of 19th century judges in cases about contracts in restraint of trade one finds lip service paid to current economic theories but if one looks at what they said in the light of what they did, one finds that they struck down a bargain if they thought it was unconscionable as between the parties to it, and upheld it if they thought it was not.'

In the same year, just before the *Schroeder* judgment was delivered in the House of Lords, Lord Denning in the *Bundy* case,[3] said:

'There are cases in our books in which the courts will set aside a contract, or a transfer of property, when the parties have not

2. [1974] 3 All ER 616.
3. *Lloyds Bank Ltd v Bundy* [1975] QB 326.

met on equal terms, when the one is so strong in bargaining power and the other so weak that, as a matter of common fairness, it is not right that the strong should be allowed to push the weak to the wall. Hitherto those exceptional cases have been treated each as a separate category in itself. But I think the time has come when we should seek to find a principle to unite them. I put on one side contracts or transactions which are voidable for fraud or misrepresentation or mistake. All those are governed by settled principles. I go along to those where there has been inequality of bargaining power, such as to merit the intervention of the court.'

Unfair Contract Terms Act 1977 (UCTA)
The second category of principal limitations and restrictions is contained in UCTA which came into force on 1 February 1978. Before examining some of the statutory provisions, the comments of Lord Wilberforce and Lord Diplock in *Photo Production Limited v Securicor Transport Ltd*[4] serve as a useful introduction. Lord Wilberforce said of UCTA:

'This Act applies to consumer contracts and those based on standard terms and enables exclusion clauses to be applied with regard to what is just and reasonable. It is significant that Parliament refrained from legislating over the whole field of contract. After this Act, in commercial matters generally, when the parties are not of an equal bargaining power, and when risks are normally borne by insurance, not only is the case for judicial intervention undemonstrated, but there is everything to be said and this seems to have been Parliament's intention, for leaving the parties free to apportion the risks as they think fit and for accepting their decisions.'

Lord Diplock contributed *inter alia* the following at p.569:

'An exclusion clause is one which excludes or modifies an obligation . . . that would otherwise arise under the contract by implication of law . . . Since the presumption is that the parties by entering into the contract intended to accept the implied obligations, exclusion clauses are to be construed strictly . . . In commercial contracts negotiated between business men capable of looking after their own interests and of deciding how risks inherent in the performance of various kinds of contracts can be most economic-

4. [1980] 1 All ER 556.

ally borne (generally by insurance), it is in my view wrong to place a strained construction on words in an exclusion clause which are clear and fairly susceptible of one meaning only . . . .'

The purpose of UCTA was to impose further limits on the extent to which civil liability for breach of contract or for negligence or other breach of duty can be avoided by contract terms or otherwise.

For the purposes of restricting liability the relevant sections are ss 2, 3, 11, 13 and Schedule 2.

Undoubtedly in contracts for electronic fund transfers the financial institution is contracting either with a consumer or on its written standard terms of business. Its ability to restrict liability for inadequate performance must be contained in a contract term which satisfies the requirement of reasonableness (s3). It is in section 11 that there is to be found a provision explaining 'reasonableness' – namely, 'the term shall have been a fair and reasonable one to be included having regard to the circumstances which were, or ought reasonably to have been known to or in the contemplation of the parties when the contract was made'. But the burden of proof that a term satisfies the requirement of reasonableness falls on those claiming that it does (s11(4)). Where a provision seeks to restrict liability to a specified sum of money and it is necessary to determine whether that provision satisfies the requirement of reasonableness, regard is to be had to the resources available to the party so seeking to restrict his liability and also 'how far it was open to him to cover himself by insurance' (s11(4)).

What is left to be implied?

The conclusion must be that in all the standard conditions of contract the terms must be reasonable and fair if they are to be effective and if Schedule 2 to UCTA is the guide, after having regard to the parties' bargaining powers and the practicalities of complying with the conditions.

Is it too late in the day to have regard to Bowen, LJ in the *Moorcook* case[5] in which he said:

'The implication which the law draws from what must obviously have been the intention of the parties, the law draws

5. (1889) 14 PD 64.

with the object of giving efficacy to the transaction and preventing such a failure of consideration as cannot have been within the contemplation of either side; and I believe if one were to take all the cases, and they are many, of implied warranties or covenants in law, it will be found that in all of them the law is raising an implication from the presumed intention of the parties with the object of giving to the transaction such effecacy as both parties must have intended that at all events it should have. In business transactions such as this, what the law desires to effect by the implication is to give such business efficacy to the transaction as must have been intended at all events by both parties who are business men; not to impose on one side all perils of the transaction, or to emancipate one side from all the chances of failure, but to make each party promise in law as much, at all events, as it must have been in the contemplation of both parties that he should be responsible for in respect of those perils of chance.'

We all remember how Scrutton, LJ expressed the point in *Reigate v Union Manufacturing Co*.[6]

'A term can only be implied if it is necessary in the business sense to give efficacy to the contract, ie, if it is such a term that it can confidently be said that if at the time the contract was being negotiated someone had said to the parties "what will happen in such a case?" they would both have replied "of course so and so will happen; we will not trouble to say that, it is too clear".'

Application to the six examples

Thus with case law and statute (UCTA) in mind let us consider our first six examples and the malfunction which has occurred.

(1) The first concerns the county council cheques. If there is fraud or mistake on the part of the customer's staff then only when the bank is aware of the mistake will it have any liability for paying away what its customer does not intend, as a result of the fraud or mistake. The customer has after all abandoned the customary banking practice of preparing in manuscript each cheque and has requested the bank to accept the mass-produced end product against an indemnity which, although in standard terms, is effectively negotiated in each case. I doubt whether the duty of the banker in relation to payments and transactions has yet extended to requiring the banker to recognise any mistake on the part of the customer

6. [1918] 1 QB 592 at 605.

and to reject a customer's apparent instruction before complying.

At present the bank is entitled to act on what the customer's machine has required to be done.

(2) In the second example the bank has misread the instructions in the telex from Singapore and is at the mercy of the customer. He can only compensate the customer for the damage and seek to recover from the party unjustly enriched. And if the telex were badly typed or ambiguous, the bank would be on enquiry to clarify the instruction before making payment.

(3) The practice of requiring a bank to act on telephone instruction is usually the result of particular negotiations in each case, again to suit the customer's business, rather than the bank's. Possibly there is equality of bargaining power and the bank will have its own conditions in mind which it hopes the customer will accept, but they are probably not standard conditions under UCTA s.3.

If the customer wishes the bank to act on its telephone instruction, then the bank must reasonably stipulate that the consequences of misunderstanding the customer's instruction are at the customer's risk. To ensure that the customer knows what the bank has done as a result, the bank gives the customer promptly a written memorandum of the action taken so that, if it is wrong, correction may be possible.

(4) The formal agreement for a cash card will provide that a card-holder 'shall keep secret his personal number (PIN) and take all reasonable care to ensure that the card is not lost, mislaid or stolen'. The bank will be entitled to debit the account of the card-holder for all cash withdrawals except those occurring after the card-holder has cancelled the agreement or after he has informed the bank of loss, unless of course the card-holder has failed to keep the number secret and the card for his personal use. These are undoubted 'standard conditions' of business within s.3 of UCTA. If the card-holder has broken the conditions the bank accepts no liability to him, and this would not seem to be challengeable under UCTA.

(5) In relation to the direct debiting system my fifth example is a 'standard indemnity', which the joining organisation is required to give to all the clearing banks and others, in consideration of those banks accepting instructions from that organisation to debit accounts of their customers, as required by the organisation from time to time.

Expressly each bank is exonerated from any duty to check or verify the direct debit instruction. The organisation agrees to indemnify on a bank's first demand against claims, and to pay forthwith the amount demanded by the bank without proof or other agreement to or by the organisation. However, if the loss or claim is caused or contributed to by the negligence of the bank, the liability of the organisation is to that extent abated.

If the debit were paid after the customer cancelled the authority to his bank to honour it, the bank can recover from the payee and the customer may expect his bank to credit his account with the amount of the unauthorised debit. If it is the organisation which has overlooked the fact that the direct debit has not been made then the customer, if disadvantaged through lapse of a policy, should have an effective claim for damages against the organisation but not against the bank for failing to see that a regular direct debit has not been made. The position might, however, be otherwise if unknown to the customer, a standing order has, in fact, been operated on a direct debit basis to suit both the bank and the organisation.

(6) In the sixth example, regard is had to the CHAPS system. CHAPS is an electronic system for sending guaranteed unconditional sterling payments with same-day value from one clearing bank to another clearing bank. As between the clearing banks the CHAPS rules govern their relationship. As between the bank and its customer the use of whatever electronic transfer system is available is not normally the subject of the banker/customer contract. The customer simply requires funds to be transferred on a particular day before a particular time to the account of a customer of another bank. He leaves it to his bank to choose a particular system to give effect to his instruction. His sole concern is that his instruction should be implemented.

If as a result of electronic failure the funds leave the bank and are not credited, can it really be said that the risk is that of the customer? There may be alternative arrangements which the bank could make to ensure that the customer's desires are met. Would it not be an unreasonable condition for the bank to excuse performance in the event of failure of the system?

Once the computer processes are set in motion, *Momm v Barclays Bank International*[7] seems to have decided,

---

7. [1977] QB 790.

H

payment is complete. It was held that payment was complete when the bank decided to accept instructions to credit the plaintiff's account and the computer processes for doing so were set in motion. Notice to the payee was not an essential ingredient of·a completed payment. Thus, as between the bank and the customer the incomplete electronic processes appear to ensure that the customer's account is reduced by the amount of the debit. If, however, same day value is not recorded for the payee and the payee seeks damages for lost interest, as between the customer and the payee, there is *prima facie* liability on the part of the customer. In meeting this liability the customer can look to his bank for compensation by way of damages naturally flowing from the breach of contract to transfer funds giving same-day value.

Effect of supervening events

What standard of facility should the customer contractually be able to expect from his banker? Is he entitled to expect the most modern alternative system to ensure payment? It has been suggested to me that it may not be easy for a banker to allege that the contract has been frustrated by supervening illegality, as when exchange control prohibits payment in the country where payment is to be made, but a declaration of war between the UK and that country would suffice. My colleague goes on that an earthquake destroying the banking system in the place of payment might well be frustration, but not where the earthquake's effect is to destroy the premises and equipment of one of the bank's correspondent banks unless the payment instruction stipulated that the correspondent bank, unfortunately destroyed, was the specified correspondent. If in some future star wars telecommunication satellites were destroyed, perhaps the banks might be expected to have an alternative system of communications. In much the same way, if the public electricity supply were to fail in a foreign financial centre that would be frustration, but not if it were the practice for the banks in question to have standby generators. Industrial disputes leading to the closure of the postal telecommunications system, or power workers' strikes leading to the failure of electronic equipment would not therefore be frustration, and payment could and should be effected by the banker by some other means. In this connection the banker/customer contract is not overtly subject to terms which purport to exempt the banks from any liability in its payments services.

Need for care in drafting

Valuable points were made in an article in the *International Financial Law Review* of October 1983 by Graham Rowbotham and Jonathan Sullivan of Simmons & Simmons. They draw attention to those cases where the bank supplies the software and a third party supplies the hardware, and the liabilities of the bank to its customer-user, particularly where the bank has selected or recommended the hardware with possible legal representations as to its suitability and subsequent servicing.

The bank would have to safeguard itself by avoiding any lax wording in explanatory material and adopt strict instructions to staff on the extent to which oral or written representations can be made to potential or existing customers.

A contractual term is suggested to the effect that a customer has not relied on any representations by the bank but has formed his or her own opinion and assessment. 'When read together with the surrounding circumstances the term might indicate that such statements as had been made were not factual but matters of opinion or that they had not been relied upon by the representee.' They suggest that banks might consider the option of seeking to limit on a reasonable basis their liability in contract for rescision or damages, and, to the extent practicable, in negligence, by the insertion of appropriate clauses in agreements to be entered into with the bank by system users.

The message to the bank must originate from the correct decision-making organ of the customer, and the mandate from a corporate customer must indicate who is authorised to give oral instructions on which the bank can rely.

The contract might provide for the presumption of the authenticity or identification of the authorised person; for example, a special code-number to be used would be known only to the originator as in the case of a cash card. The reasonableness of stipulations as to non-disclosure of an individual's personal identity number should be undoubted, and the use of a number for a corporate customer might perhaps be protected by having the number in two parts, one being known by one official and the other by another. The advent of electronic communication and the terms upon which it is made are a further step away from the written instruction towards the personal direct and active contact. Perhaps the movement away from written instruction is a return to the advice of George Rae in 1885 in *The Country Banker* (page 188) when he discouraged the banker from writing to his customer and encouraged oral contact in these cases:

'In your intercourse with your clients, you will find a safe observance, never to discuss with a customer the position of his account by letter, if you can by any means arrange to do so by word of mouth. If the discussion has to be of an unpleasant cast, the mere putting it in writing will give to your missive a formality and bite of their own.

'Let us say that you have written to a man to reduce or pay off his account; you have probably heard something to his disadvantage, but you cannot well say so in writing, or give your authority. He has no chance, therefore, of confuting the charge, because you do not give it him to confute; whereas, if you had a friendly talk with him, freed from the constraint of putting everything into writing, he might be able to disabuse your mind of what may be rankling there to his prejudice. It is at least certain that a man will reveal more of his mind to you, in ten minutes' talk, in the seclusion of your private office, than he will ever be able to express or put his hand to in writing...'

Whatever the changes, the basic position is one between the originator of a request for action and the recipient of that request who undertakes the action directly or indirectly. Apart from its authenticity, the essence of a valid transaction must be the identification of the amount, the payee, and the time and place of transfer and any other conditions to be observed by a banker before a payment or other action is undertaken.

Electronic funds transfer – the speculative future

I have not mentioned EFTPOS as a source of malfunction. Under this system a bank customer in a shop uses a plastic card to pay for things by means of a direct debit to his account, giving rise to an immediate credit in the shopkeeper's bank account. The direct debiting takes effect in the shop at the check-out or till and the payment is only possible if the customer has credit funds with the bank to meet the purchase, or the intended debit is within the scope of a lending facility. What could be simpler?

If the bank customer wishes to be able to pay for goods in this way he will enter into an agreement with his bank in the knowledge that, as in the case of credit cards, a large number of retailers will have a separate agreement with the bank, indicating their readiness to be paid in this way. Contract, all the way!

US Electronic Funds Transfer Act, 1978

In the US, however, the view was taken that legislation was necessary and Congress passed in 1978 the 'Electronic Funds Transfer Act'. The purpose of the legislation was 'to provide a basic framework establishing the rights, liabilities and responsibilities of participants in electronic funds transfer systems'. The primary object was the provision of individual consumer rights. In the Act the term 'Electronic Funds Transfer' was to mean 'any transfer of funds other than a transaction originated by check, draft or similar paper instrument, which is initiated through an electronic terminal, telephonic instrument, or computer or magnetic tape, so as to order, instruct or authorise a financial institution to debit or credit an account'. The term was to include point of sale transfers. The Board of Governors of the Federal Reserve System were to prescribe regulations and issue model clauses for optional use by financial institutions. This statute, however, stipulated that the terms and conditions of electronic funds transfers should be disclosed in readily understandable language and should include the customer's liability for unauthorised transfers and, ideally, the advisability of prompt reporting of any loss, theft or any unauthorised use of a card or other means of access, and, significantly, the consumer's right to stop payment to a pre-authorised electronic funds transfer, and the procedure to be followed to initiate such a stop-payment order. Provisions were made for periodic statements and a specific provision governs the ability of a consumer to stop a pre-authorised transfer by notifying the financial institution up to three business days preceding the schedule date of transfer. Of particular interest to us are the provisions contained in sections 908 and 909 entitled 'Error Resolution' and 'Consumer Liability for Unauthorised Transfers' respectively.

If a customer within sixty days of receipt of a statement points out to the financial institution an error in the document and the amount involved, the financial institution is duty bound to investigate and report. If it cannot complete its investigation within ten days it may provisionally recredit the consumer and conclude its inquiry, within forty-five days. The error, if confirmed by investigation, must be corrected within one business day after the result of the investigation.

If no error is disclosed, then within eight days of concluding the inquiry the explanation of the findings are to be given to the consumer.

If in proceedings the court finds that there was no investigation in good faith or that the financial institution did not have a reasonable basis for concluding there was no error, the consumer is entitled to treble damages.

Section 909 deals with the consumer's liability for unauthorised transfers and echoes our own Consumer Credit Act 1974, which in s.83 provides that in the event of any loss of a credit card the card-holder's subsequent liability is terminated when he has notified the financial institution concerned – and his liability before such notice, which can be oral, is limited to £30 (£50 on and after 20th May 1985).

In the US statute, a consumer's liability for unauthorised transfer shall in no event exceed the lesser of $50 or the actual cash or value of services obtained prior to notifying the financial institution of unauthorised transfer. Reimbursement to a consumer need not be made if the consumer has not notified the unauthorised transfers within sixty days of 'transmittal of the statement' and the financial institution establishes that the losses would not otherwise have occurred. Similarly, reimbursement is not required in the case of loss or theft if the consumer is dilatory in notifying the financial institution and does not do so within two business days and the financial institution establishes that the loss would not otherwise have occurred within two business days: the consumer's liability is not to exceed $500 in any proceedings and the burden of proof is on the financial institution to show that the transfer is authorised.

In the United Kingdom in relation to stolen credit cards and cheque books with cheque cards, we do not have a system which enables us to state that losses would not have been incurred had the consumer notified us promptly. Our system is such at present that the continued use by a criminal of a credit card is difficult to prevent.

Possible reasonable restrictions or undertaking a restricted service

What valid and binding restrictions upon liability can the banker reasonably impose on those using electronic devices to activate transfers and withdrawals from their bank accounts?

To impose a duty of care upon the customer as regards his custody of the plastic card or his personal identification number or the code to operate the system would not fall foul of s.13 of UCTA. If the customer is careless and notifies the bank of his carelessness then the bank can undertake to take all reasonable steps to minimise the loss to the customer.

The banker should be clear in what he undertakes to do, so that the need for any restriction on liability or exemption does not arise: ie, 'If you the customer are careful in your custody of the know-how, and exercise skill and care in operating the machinery, we the bank will implement your instructions to transfer moneys and pay cash to you'. It must be appreciated that s.13 appears to outlaw terms or conditions which 'exclude or restrict the relevant obligation or duty' which are included in a bank's written standard terms of business.

Lastly, it should be reasonable to expect that power failures and industrial disputes by third parties, which interrupt normal banking services, are regarded as lawful excuses for non-performance by the banker. It is preferable that such excuses are set out in express contractual terms, but there may be valid argument that such excuses are of no avail to the bank if alternative action to provide an equivalent service could have been taken by the bank in question, or by the average bank with which comparison could be made.

APPENDIX

Electronic Funds Transfer Act 1978, P.L. 95–630, 15 USC 1693

908 Error resolution

(a) If a financial institution, within sixty days after having transmitted to a consumer documentation pursuant to section 906(a), (c), or (d) or notification pursuant to section 906(b), receives oral or written notice in which the consumer:
  (1) sets forth or otherwise enables the financial institution to identify the name and account number of the consumer;
  (2) indicates the consumer's belief that the documentation, or in the case of notification pursuant to section 906(b), the consumer's account, contains an error and the amount of such error; and
  (3) sets forth the reasons for the consumer's belief (where applicable) that an error has occurred;
  the financial institution shall investigate the alleged error, determine whether an error has occurred and report or mail the results of such investigation and determination to the consumer within ten business days. The financial institution may require written confirmation to be provided to it within ten business days of an oral notification of error if, when the oral notification is made, the consumer is advised of such requirement and the address to which such confirmation should be sent. A financial institution which requires written confirmation in accordance with the previous sentence need not provisionally recredit a consumer's account in accordance with subsection (c), nor shall the financial institution be liable under subsection (a) if that written confirmation is not received within the ten-day period referred to in the previous sentence.

(b) If the financial institution determines that an error did occur, it shall promptly, but in no event more than one business day after such determination, correct the error subject to section 909, including the crediting of interest where applicable.

(c) If a financial institution receives notice of an error in the manner and within the time period specified in subsection (a), it may, in lieu of the requirements of subsections (a) and (b), within ten business days after receiving such notice provisionally recredit the consumer's account for the amount alleged to be in error, subject to section 909, including interest where

applicable, pending the conclusion of its investigation and its determination of whether an error has occurred. Such investigation shall be concluded not later than forty-five days after receipt of notice of the error. During the pendency of the investigation, the consumer shall have full use of the funds provisionally recredited.
(d) If the financial institution determines after its investigation pursuant to subsection (a) or (c) that an error did not occur, it shall deliver or mail to the consumer an explanation of its findings within eight business days after the conclusion of its investigations, and upon request of the consumer promptly deliver or mail to the consumer reproductions of all documents which the financial institution relied on to conclude that such error did not occur. The financial institution shall include notice of the right to request reproductions with the explanation of its findings.
(e) If in any action under section 915, the court finds that:
  (1) the financial institution did not provisionally recredit a consumer's account within the ten-day period specified in subsection (c), and the financial institution (A) did not make a good faith investigation of the alleged error, or (B) did not have a reasonable basis for believing that the consumer's account was not in error; or
  (2) the financial institution knowingly and willfully concluded that the consumer's account was not in error when such conclusion could not reasonably have been drawn from the evidence available to the financial institution at the time of its investigation,
then the consumer shall be entitled to treble damages determined under section 915(a)(1).
(f) For the purpose of this section, an error consists of:
  (1) an unauthorised electronic fund transfer;
  (2) an incorrect electronic fund transfer from or to the consumer's account;
  (3) the omission from a periodic statement of an electronic fund transfer affecting the consumer's account which should have been included;
  (4) a computational error by the financial institution;
  (5) the consumer's receipt of an incorrect amount of money from an electronic terminal;
  (6) a consumer's request for additional information or clarification concerning an electronic fund transfer or any documentation required by this title; or
  (7) any other error described in regulations of the Board.

909 Consumer liability for unauthorised transfers

(a) A consumer shall be liable for any unauthorised electronic fund transfer involving the account of such consumer only if the card or other means of access utilised for such transfer was an accepted card or other means of access and if the issuer of such card, code, or other means of access has provided a means whereby the user of such card, code, or other means of access can be identified as the person authorised to use it, such as by signature, photograph, or fingerprint or by electronic or mechanical confirmation. In no event, however, shall a consumer's liability for an unauthorised transfer exceed the lesser of:
(1) $50, or
(2) the amount of money or value of property or services obtained in such unauthorised electronic fund transfer prior to the time the financial institution is notified of, or otherwise becomes aware of, circumstances which lead to the reasonable belief that an unauthorised electronic fund transfer involving the consumer's account has been or may be effected. Notice under this paragraph is sufficient when such steps have been taken as may be reasonably required in the ordinary course of business to provide the financial institution with the pertinent information, whether or not any particular officer, employee, or agent of the financial institution does in fact receive such information.
Notwithstanding the foregoing, reimbursement need not be made to the consumer for losses the financial institution establishes would not have occurred but for the failure of the consumer to report within sixty days of transmittal of the statement (or in extenuating circumstances such as extended travel or hospitalisation, within a reasonable time under the circumstances) any unauthorised electronic fund transfer or account error which appears on the periodic statement provided to the consumer under section 906. In addition, reimbursement need not be made to the consumer for losses which the financial institution establishes would not have occurred but for the failure of the consumer to report any loss or theft of a card or other means of access within two business days after the consumer learns of the loss or theft (or inextenuating circumstances such as extended travel or hospitalisation, within a longer period which is reasonable under the

circumstances), but the consumer's liability under this subsection in any such case may not exceed a total of $500, or the amount of unauthorised electronic fund transfers which occur following the close of two business days (or such longer period) after the consumer learns of the loss or theft but prior to the financial institution under this subsection, whichever is less.
(b) In any action which involves a consumer's liability for an unauthorised electronic fund transfer, the burden of proof is upon the financial institution to show that the electronic fund transfer was authorised or, if the electronic fund transfer was unauthorised, then the burden of proof is upon the financial institution to establish that the conditions of liability set forth in subsection (a) have been met, and, if the transfer was initiated after the effective date of section 905, that the disclosures required to be made to the consumer under section 905 (a) (1) and (2) were in fact made in accordance with such section.
(c) In the event of a transaction which involves both an unauthorised electronic fund transfer and an extension of credit as defined in section 103 (e) *(15 USC 1602)* of this Act pursuant to an agreement between the consumer and the financial institution to extend such credit to the consumer in the event the consumer's account is overdrawn, the limitation on the consumer's liability for such transaction shall be determined solely in accordance with this section.
(d) Nothing in this section imposes liability upon a consumer for an unauthorised electronic fund transfer in excess of his liability for such a transfer under other applicable law or under any agreement with the consumer's financial institution.
(e) Except as provided in this section, a consumer incurs no liability from an unauthorised electronic fund transfer.

UNFAIR CONTRACT TERMS ACT 1977
Avoidance of liability for negligence, breach of contract, etc
Negligence liability
2. (1) A person cannot by reference to any contract term or to a notice given to persons generally or to particular persons exclude or restrict his liability for death or personal injury resulting from negligence.
   (2) In the case of other loss or damage, a person cannot so exclude or restrict his liability for negligence except in so far as the term or notice satisfies the requirement of reasonableness.

(3) Where a contract term or notice purports to exclude or restrict liability for negligence a person's agreement to or awareness of it is not of itself to be taken as indicating his voluntary acceptance of any risk.

Liability arising in contract
3. (1) This section applies as between contracting parties where one of them deals as consumer or on the other's written standard terms of business.
   (2) As against that party, the other cannot by reference to any contract term:
      (a) when himself in breach of contract, exclude or restrict any liability of his in respect of the breach; or
      (b) claim to be entitled:
         (i) to render a contractual performance substantially different from that which was reasonably expected of him;
         or
         (ii) in respect of the whole or any part of his contractual obligation, to render no performance at all;
   except in so far as (in any of the cases mentioned above in this subsection) the contract term satisfies the requirement of reasonableness.

PART 1 Explanatory provisions

The 'reasonableness test'
11. (1) In relation to a contract term, the requirement of reasonableness for the purposes of this Part of this Act, section 3 of the Misrepresentation Act 1967 and section 3 of the Misrepresentation Act (Northern Ireland) 1967 is that the term shall have been a fair and reasonable one to be included having regard to the circumstances which were, or ought reasonably to have been, known to or in the contemplation of the parties when the contract was made.
    (2) In determining for the purposes of section 6 or 7 above whether a contract term satisfies the requirement of reasonableness, regard shall be had in particular to the matters specified in Schedule 2 to this Act; but this subsection does not prevent the court or arbitrator from holding, in accordance with any rule of law, that a term which purports to exclude or restrict any relevant liability is not a term of the contract.

(3) In relation to a notice (not being a notice having contractual effect), the requirement of reasonableness to allow reliance on it, having regard to all the circumstances obtaining when the liability arose or (but for the notice) would have arisen.

(4) Where by reference to a contract term or notice a person seeks to restrict liability to a specified sum of money, and the question arises (under this or any other Act) whether the term or notice satisfies the requirement of reasonableness, regard shall be had in particular (but without prejudice to subsection (2) above in the case of contract terms) to:
  (a) the resources which he could expect to be available to him for the purpose of meeting the liability should it arise; and
  (b) how far it was open to him to cover himself by insurance.

(5) It is for those claiming that a contract term or notice satisfies the requirement of reasonableness to show that it does.

13. (1) To the extent that this Part of this Act prevents the exclusion or restriction of any liability it also prevents:
  (a) making the liability or its enforcement subject to restrictive or onerous conditions;
  (b) excluding or restricting any right or remedy in respect of the liability, or subjecting a person to any prejudice in consequence of his pursuing any such right or remedy;
  (c) excluding or restricting rules of evidence or procedure;
  and (to that extent) sections 2 and 5 to 7 also prevent excluding or restricting liability by reference to terms and notices which exclude or restrict the relevant obligation or duty.

(2) But an agreement in writing to submit present or future differences to arbitration is not to be treated under this Part of the Act as excluding or restricting any liability.

SCHEDULE 2

'Guidelines' for application of reasonableness test

Sections 11 (2) and 24 (2)

The matters to which regard is to be had in particular for the purposes of sections 6 (3), 7 (3) and (4), 20 and 21 are any of the following which appear to be relevant:
(a) the strength of the bargaining positions of the parties relative to each other, taking into account (among other things) alternative means by which the customer's requirements could have been met;

(b) whether the customer received an inducement to agree to the term, or in accepting it had an opportunity of entering into a similar contract with other persons, but without having to accept a similar term;
(c) whether the customer knew or ought reasonably to have known the existence and extent of the term (having regard, among other things, to any custom of the trade and any previous course of dealing between the parties);
(d) where the term excludes or restricts any relevant liability if some condition is not complied with, whether it was reasonable at the time of the contract to expect that compliance with that condition would be practicable;
(e) whether the goods were manufactured, processed or adapted to the special order of the customer.

THE ELECTRONIC PRESENTATION OF INSTRUMENTS
The Truncation of Cheques and Other Negotiable and Non-Negotiable Instruments Through EFT

Anu Arora

The tremendous increase in the volume of paper-based transactions cleared by the banks has led not only to the increased automation of the clearing and payments procedure, but also to the substitution of methods of payment and the separation of the clearing systems which accommodate the different types of payments systems. The purpose of this paper is to examine the extent to which the existing methods of payment may be adapted to cope with the increasingly large volume of paper-based payments being made through the banking system by the electronic presentation of data, so that a payment may be made without the actual physical presentation of the instrument. It is intended to examine, particularly, the simplification of the cheque or debit clearing by cheque truncation and to explore the extent to which cheques and other paper-based methods of payment may be made more efficiently by the transmission of relevant data so that payment may be made without the physical presentation of the instrument itself.

The clearing system

Presently, there are some four or five different clearing systems for the payment of cheques, credit transfers, standing orders, direct debits and BACS. Many of the payments made by these various methods can originate from and be directed to anywhere in the country, and because on the whole the present clearing systems are based on the physical presentation to the paying bank of the instrument evidencing the right to payment, it takes up to four days for the payment process to be completed. This undoubtedly results in a waste of time and resources; there are limits to the economies that can be achieved when inter-bank cheque clearing is based on the physical movement of paper.

The general and town clearing systems handle the vast majority of items being presented for payment within the banking system (the general clearing systems in 1980 handled approximately 1,454 million inter-bank transfers valued at £405,690 million and the town clearing system handled an estimated five million items valued at approximately £4,051,203 million).

The general clearing
The general clearing takes place only once each working day. The provincial branches of collecting banks forward articles for collection to their respective London head offices and presentation of cheques and other articles for payment is made by the London head office to the London head offices of the respective banks on which they are drawn. The deliveries must be made as early as possible to allow articles to be checked and sorted by the drawee banks' head offices and all articles presented on any day must be presented by 11.30 am. All the cheques and articles presented must be listed by amount and the docket accompanying each batch of cheques must state the total amount of cheques in the batch and the name of the collecting bank. The cheques and articles are handed to the paying bank by this time for final delivery.

During the afternoon the paying bank will check through all the cheques presented to it for payment by the different banks. The cheques go through the reader-sorter machines which will check the amount and number of each cheque and ensure that they correspond with the list prepared by the collecting bank. Once this is checked by the computer and accepted as correct, it will debit the drawer's account with the amount of the cheque.

Any cheques which are incorrectly listed or presented to the wrong bank for payment are rejected by the reader-sorter machine. The clerks at the paying bank go through these cheques, which are once again made up into bundles for returning to the bank which presented them for payment. Such rejected cheques have to be returned to the collecting bank by the following day by 8.15 am, and are charged by the returning bank to the presenting bank. A final agreement of 'in' and 'out' clearing totals is then agreed by the collecting and paying banks, including any wrongly delivered cheques; this is done at 10.30 am on the working day following the day when the cheques were presented. The daily settlement sheet is then signed on behalf of the banks showing the total of the cheques presented for payment by them respectively on the previous day, less the total of returned items. A final settlement then takes place between all the clearing banks on the totals they are to receive or pay, and the net balances are transferred between the accounts kept by the banks at the Bank of

England at 4.30 pm on the working day following the day of presentation.

The articles which are paid in this way are then sent by the drawee bank's London head office to the branch banks where the drawer's accounts are kept. If the drawer's branch is to dishonour the cheque (eg, because payment has been countermanded), this must be done by returning the article on the day the branch bank receives it or if the need to return is inadvertently overlooked, on the following day, but in these circumstances notice of intention to dishonour must be given by telephone to the payee's branch bank by midday on that day. The amount of the dishonoured article, which has already been included in the settlement between the presenting and drawee banks, is then recovered by the branch sending an unpaid claim form to its head office accompanied by the article, and this is then delivered to the collecting bank through the clearing like an ordinary cheque and is paid in the same way. Since the article will already have been paid to the collecting bank by this time, the effect of the collecting bank paying the amount of the unpaid claim form is in effect to cancel the original payment. An answer must be written on each article returned with the unpaid claim form showing why the article was dishonoured.

The debit clearing .

A similar system is in operation for payments made under the credit clearing system but once again it normally takes four days for items to be cleared and paid. The credit transfer system may be used for several purposes; for example, the payment of salaries, commercial invoices, payment of bills etc, and handles over 235 million paper vouchers per annum. The credit transfer form may be prepared in several different ways, namely by hand, typewriter, accounting machine, address plate or computer printer, with the result that there is no single method by which automation techniques can be applied and no uniformity in the credit transfer forms passed between banks.

Cheque truncation

The banks, therefore, need to solve the problems of, and which arise from, the physical movement of paper in the clearing process. To a limited extent this has already been achieved by a process known as truncation which involves the capture of relevant data to enable payment to be made to the payee's account, and simultaneously for the drawer's account to be debited, without the physical movement of paper. At present this can only be done when the drawer and payee of a cheque have accounts at different branches of the same bank; a cheque drawn on the branch of another bank still has to be physically presented for clearing.

A problem with the cheque truncation system is that of capturing the relevant data for electronic transmission. This may be resolved in one of two ways, namely: in a partially truncated system cheques could be remitted to the clearing department for data collection with cheques being retained at a central location; the cheque is not then sent on to the branch where the drawer has his account. Alternatively, in a fully developed system the data collection would be carried out at the collecting branch with cheques being retained at that branch. In the latter case the branch to which the cheque is presented for collection will truncate it by capturing the relevant information on computer tape which is sent to the bank's head office so that the details of the accounts which have to be credited/debited may be entered on the records of the drawer's and payee's accounts.

If cheque truncation were fully implemented for inter-bank payments there would be an instant reduction in the volume of paper handled within the clearing system, and eventually with full automation it would be possible to provide for the payment of cheques, credit transfers and other instruments by appropriate payment messages being sent through CHAPS. The data necessary for the electronic payment of money (namely the payee's name and account number, bank and branch codes, together with the payee's name and account number with his bank and branch codes, and the amount of the payment) could be captured at one of two following stages:

(i) since the cheque already has magnetic inkprints giving details of the bank and branch codes and account number on which payment is to be made, the cashier at the counter of the collecting bank may key into the computer additional information (for example the amount of the cheque, the payee's account and other details) so that its computer can transmit the information and receive payment; or

(ii) the same information is keyed in by the cashier when the cheque is paid in for collection and may be encoded later at the branch of the collecting bank so that it never leaves the branch of the bank which received it for collection.

If fully implemented the process of cheque truncation may be completed by the cashier at the counter of the collecting bank when the cheque is paid in. The cashier will pass the cheque through the document reader machine which transmits the data on the cheque to the bank's computer. The cashier will also key in any further information necessary and each transaction will be given its own individual reference number. A complete record of the transaction in question is then transmitted electronically to the paying banks, including the individual reference number. Where the paying bank refuses payment, for example when the account on which the cheque is drawn has insufficient funds, the paying bank will be able to refuse payment by sending a reverse payment message to the collecting bank by using its own computer terminal. The reference number given to each individual transaction can be used in these circumstances to identify the transaction in question.

In order to extend the cheque truncation process for interbank payment, the banks will have to settle certain issues, for example there would have to be reciprocal arrangements with responsibility for the technical regularity of cheques being on the bank which receives them for collection.

The truncation process could be extended to other instruments which have presently to be presented physically for collection, for example credit transfer forms; but this in the first instance would require the standardisation of credit transfer vouchers.

Advantages

There are several advantages to the introduction of cheque truncation on a wider basis. It would remove the need for several separate listings, the physical movement of paper at the clearing house, returning wrong deliveries or sending a dishonoured cheque to the collecting branch. The major task of handling paper would disappear resulting in a speedier and more economical method of payment. More importantly the delay of four days before payment is made under the present clearing of cheques and credit payments would no longer exist, resulting in a 'paper-based' system of payment which is more competitive with the totally automated systems of payment eg, point of sale.

Cheque truncation overseas

Whilst the banks in the United Kingdom have not yet resolved fully the problems of truncation the automation of cheque clearing is fairly advanced in Europe. In France and West Germany, as between banks in the same country, the Eurocheque is not physically presented for payment, but the cheque data is transmitted on magnetic tape to the paying bank. It is eventually contemplated that the necessary data will be communicated by direct telecommunication to the paying bank.

Germany also has an international arrangement of this kind with Austria, the Netherlands, Norway, Spain, Sweden and Switzerland for the payment of German Eurocheques. One of the problems which such an international arrangement has to resolve is the variety of national code lines on cheques, which prevent cheques being identified electronically. This may be resolved by the use of electronic reading machines which are able to decode different national code lines, or alternatively by harmonising such codes.

Some problems

A cheque is a negotiable instrument and as such can be indorsed in favour of third parties. Consequently, a method of truncation which simply records the data on the face of instrument, eg, the date, amount and payee's account number and name, is insufficient to enable payment to be made of indorsed cheques. An image of both the front and back of the cheque would be necessary and is likely to prove expensive.

One of the problems to cheque truncation in the USA is that cheques are returned to the customer after payment has been made against them. A number of banks have introduced a different method of cheque truncation to the one operating in the UK and Europe. The bank customer is supplied with chequebooks which make a carbonless copy of each cheque as it is written. The original is used for payment and the copy retained by the customer. The bank does not return the cancelled cheque after payment has been made, but the customer is sent periodic bank statements which he can check against his retained copy of the cheques he has drawn.

The one disadvantage of cheque truncation is that there is no verification of the drawer's signature on a cheque because it is never seen by anyone at the branch on which it is drawn. The only protection against forged or unauthorised cheques is the drawer's own comparison of the periodic statements of account sent to him by his bank with his own record of cheque drawings.

THE ELECTRONIC PRESENTATION AND TRANSFER OF SHIPPING DOCUMENTS

Alan Urbach

Trade and transportation documents as stores of value

Shipping documents, most especially the bill of lading, have value in themselves in that they represent the documents of title. They also have value in the information which they contain. Errors may lead to delays in delivery which can mean demurrage charges, lost sales and even confiscation of the goods. If the information shipping documents contain becomes available to competitors, it may also lead to losses. These documents also have value through their physical presence in that not having the correct one in the right place may cause delays or losses. And yet, with the increasing complexities of international trade, correct documents have even less chance today of being in the right place at the right time than ever before. This is despite soaring expenditure in time and money on just the processing of paper.

For these reasons, shipowners, cargo buyers and sellers and their banks have all wished for some way in which documents could be more efficiently and safely handled. To most people this means electronic transmission of shipping documents. However, despite a critically recognised need, transportation (with the exception of airline passenger reservations) is probably the least automated of industries. How can this be and what is being done about it?

An industry problem

The first reasons are obvious. Transportation, both domestic and international, is a highly fragmented industry in which many participants have neither the money, the knowledge or the ability to automate. Half of the industry, air transportation, railways and the road hauliers, are over-regulated while the other half, shipowners, show the effects of individual decision-making carried to an extreme. Transportation, as an old industry, is also burdened with too many people and many wrong ways of using them. Finally, transportation has the unfortunate habit of crossing political borders, bringing in the whole unhappy panoply of customs, exchange control and government bureaucracy. It is not surprising that trade and transportation documents and their problems have multiplied, especially as the interests of the carrier and the cargo owner and their banks, like the land and sea, rarely match.

Historical solutions

When cargo buyers travelled with their ships, and often even captained them, there was no doubt as to who should receive the goods at discharge. A single notation as to the nature and quantity of goods taken on board was sufficient to establish the shipowner's liability for 'delivery (of that cargo) in like good order and well conditioned' at the port of discharge. When merchants began staying in their shops or at least taking faster ways home it became harder for the master to know to whom he was to discharge a cargo; anyone might claim that 'his ship had come in'.

To cope with this problem, masters and shipowners began to modify an idea first advanced in the small Adriatic port of Trani three years before William the Conqueror set about his reorganisation of English common law. The Ordinances of Trani required that the master enter a description of goods loaded on board to be noted in a Ship's Register. This special log came to be known as a Book of Lading (B/L). By ripping out the appropriate page and giving it to the seller the exporter gained a receipt for his goods which he could exchange with the importer for payment and which the importer in turn could show to the ship's master. Even if the buyer's face were unknown, the master's signature on the piece of paper he himself had torn out – a bill of lading – was not. From this grew the idea that specially torn pieces of paper could represent title over goods in transit. This title could even be transferred to another by signing and physically delivering the bill of lading over to that other person. In this way the negotiable bill of lading was born.

Banks too seized upon this idea. A merchant could travel with a letter from his bank promising the reader that if he delivered over the bill of lading to the bank he would be paid on behalf of the buyer. Banks felt secure in this practice as they knew that if the buyer could not present the bill of lading the captain would not hand over his purchases. And if the captain did allow discharge, then the bill of lading holder, in this case the bank, could sue the captain and through him the shipowner not only for the value of the goods but for any consequential damage suffered by the B/L holder as well. This is because delivery to the wrong party, by definition anyone other than the B/L holder, was akin to stealing. Called the tort of conversion in the UK, an action can be brought by the holder for up to six years after the event as opposed to an action in relation to the B/L itself which is time barred after one year under Hague/Hague-Visby Rules. In other countries the time in which to bring a suit may be even longer.

A modern mess

This paper-intensive process worked well when, slowly as the documents might travel in a horseman's sack or by mail packet, the cargo ship moved even more slowly. Today, even jet propelled couriers cannot move the documents quickly enough, so complicated have some multiple sales transactions become. This is particularly the case with liquid bulk cargoes. Complicated too have become government regulations and the demands from so many parties and their agents, especially banks, to see, hold, check and modify seaborne trade documents.

The easiest way to reduce the demands of paper is to be rid of the paper. We have seen that in many areas of banking this is becoming the norm. Why is it not the case with trade and transport documents?

Some reasons

Firstly, numerous national and international transportation conventions require that cargo documents be signed, although they are less clear as to whether the documents must actually be in writing or as to how the signing is to be accomplished. The latest Hamburg Rules allow for a signature to be made autobiographically, by any mechanical means such as a rubber stamp or electronically, but the convention does not seem to get away from the idea that the signature must be affixed to a real physical thing which a judge might see and touch. Secondly, even where there is no 'law', banks and customs authorities have created set rules of procedure which have the same impact as law. And thirdly, how many people would really like to arrange multi-million dollar sales on just oral agreements? For trade and transport purposes paper documents would seem to be sacrosanct.

Early efforts

The first attack on the B/L was in its role as a store of value. In the late 1800s some European grain merchants had a good idea. Why not consign the goods to a named person who would receive the cargo? If that person merely identified himself to the captain or train-master (as most of these shipments were then by rail) the master would be obliged to hand over the goods. The major advantage of this idea was that the buyer did not have to wait to receive a special document with which to identify himself. This was also the biggest disadvantage, in that the seller lost his best way of compelling a buyer to pay.

With a telegraph message now sufficient to alert the buyer, the waybill idea found little favour with the banks, but it did with some transport operators who were happy to avoid liability for misdelivery. One such group, the air freight industry, dealt itself out of the negotiable bill of lading altogether and into the easier to handle and less onerous airway bill by international convention.

The waybill clearly lends itself to electronics because it serves only as a record and not as a store of information. As such, questions as to the validity and authenticity of an electronic message about a waybill are much less severe than they are of a B/L.

Computerising the waybill

Atlantic Container Lines (ACL) and Professor Gronfors of the University of Gotenberg have taken this thought a step further. On the North Atlantic, container cargoes move mainly between sister companies. For these cargo buyers and sellers obtaining documents more quickly in order to clear goods faster is far more important than being able to finance or trade them while still on the high seas. Once the consignor has agreed to the loading information, an electronic representation of a waybill, called a DataLading passes through ACL's computer system from loading port to discharge port.

Unfortunately, bank financing is still very important for many buyers on the North Atlantic and even more so elsewhere. Many sellers also prefer to retain some control over the goods until they are paid. To allow for this Professor Gronfors introduced the Cargo Key Receipt which is still a waybill but with one important difference – the NODISP clause. With this clause the bill can be made in the name of one person, let us say the financing bank, but this named party retains a power to dispose of it to one other, the true buyer, provided he pays, or a receiver if he does not. With knowledge, time and practice, and the change in the type of documents which a bank may accept under a letter of credit under the new UCP for documentary credits, DataFreight type systems should become the preferred way for documenting most containerised freight.

Other issues

There are three drawbacks to the ACL system which prevent it from being the perfect electronic solution for handling all types of trade and transport documents.

One is that it is a closed system using ACL ports and ACL ships. This should offer a competitive advantage to ACL, which must be one reason why they are offering DataFreight. It is also why other transportation companies are looking at similar ideas, like the one being offered by GEISCO-East Asiatic. But there are other ports and places where the documentation problems may be even more acute such as at customs barriers on autobahns.

The DataFreight system is closed in a second way in that there are more people in a port than just the buyer and his bank. There are also road hauliers, port and forwarding agents, etc and there are governmental bodies such as customs. As an integrated multi-modal transportation operator ACL can provide many but not all of these services while still using the same documents and computer. This provides a competitive advantage for ACL, but what does a cargo buyer do when confronted by the documentary requirements of some of the etceteras, for example cargo insurers, customs and foreign exchange and port authorities, etc?

Efforts to modernise the system

To deal directly with this wider group of people, the US National Committee of International Trade Procedures (NCITD), which is the American version of a European SITPRO, came up with the Cargo Data Interchange System – CARDIS. Their goal was to bring everybody in the port into one electronic system. But universal systems must overcome three critical hurdles: they must use standard forms, on standard systems and in a standard way.

Full standardisation would mean that any concerned party could access the system to add or use information as needed without having to create any new documents or hold up the flow of information to others.

CARDIS tried to design just such a set of standard documents. These have not been accepted – nor have any others – because most people feel that their own solutions best solve their own problems. As a result the standardisation process has been long and difficult, and still has not been resolved. The same is equally true for systems. Few people would readily throw out their old computer and its expensive software just for a new twist. It is even more difficult to define set procedures between multiple companies and countries although efforts are proceeding in Europe.

While an essentially good idea, CARDIS has not yet generated the energy needed to persuade people that they would benefit more than they might lose by all doing things the same way. However, it is now being promoted by the Western Union Company and may yet achieve the goal of a totally paperless cargo system acceptable to all parties in the port.

Shortcomings of the waybill

CARDIS started with the idea of using only the waybill but later allowed for the use of the B/L. This is important because under the Hague Rules shippers have the right to demand a negotiable bill of lading and even under the ACL system only the DataLading is offered as a potentially 'better' substitute; one may demand a B/L or get it anyway if there is some problem with the cargo description. This is the third problem for the DataFreight system. Of course Hague could be modified, as in a sense it was for the air freight industry, but as that was in the pre-computer era they had the excuse that documents could not possibly arrive before the aeroplane, perhaps not even with it. Besides the long time it would take to change an international convention and the associated national laws there are some shippers and consignees who still would not favour getting rid of the negotiable B/L.

Two such groups are the banks and various national governments, especially in developing countries which have developed the increasingly incorrect idea that only the negotiable bill of lading and a letter of credit protects their interest or that of their customers. These groups must eventually change their minds. Certainly the new UCP will help.

One other group very much needs a title which may be freely transferred by endorsement without being subject to an underlying contract. Commodity traders, and this now includes most consignees and consignors, actively trade most types of bulk cargoes, most especially mineral and edible oils. As oil and its derivatives make up about 50 per cent of seaborne trade the needs of this group must be met as much as the DataFreight system meets the needs of general cargoes.

SeaDocs – a possible compromise

SeaDocs – Seaborne Trade Documentation System – which was

THE ELECTRONIC PRESENTATION AND TRANSFER OF SHIPPING DOCUMENTS

first proposed by the late Mr Per Gram, a noted Norwegian maritime lawyer and Chairman of the INTERTANKO Documentary Committee, and was later developed at the Chase Manhattan Bank by the author, tries to come to grips with the ACL system's third problem; what to do about multiple traded cargoes.

An analysis of the SeaDocs concept will elucidate how the system works and will help illustrate some of the other problems which must be overcome before we can have an acceptable, effective, industry-wide system for the electronic presentation and transfer of shipping documents.

What is the special problem for bulk cargoes? As oil companies, petrochemical companies and other mass raw material processors and sellers struggle to balance their production, sales and transportation units over vast distances and in the face of a constantly changing political and economic environment, they have had to resort to juggling the inputs, ie, selling the bulk cargoes while they are still on the high seas, in pipelines or even still in the ground.

The normal terms of sale for oil provide for 30 days payment. This means that the documents, including the bill of lading, will be delivered in exchange for payment 30 days after the date of the B/L, ie, the loading date. As a matter of convenience however, the documents may be sent to the buyer before payment date. This will be the case when the seller trusts the buyer and wishes to help him clear customs and of course, to facilitate the master in releasing the goods. The cargo of oil itself may have been sold twenty times before it was actually lifted out of the ground. It might be sold another ten or more times on the high seas. The sales themselves may be in different parcels from what was loaded or even scheduled to have been loaded and sometimes they may be subject to different contractual or financing terms, including, if it is even considered, different points as to when title is intended to have passed. This is especially the case if one or more intermediate buyers is being financed, as at that point the bank through its letter of credit agreement will also be trying to control the passage of title.

Add to this example that the tanker carrying the oil may need only one or two days to reach the discharge port and that it may take the terminal operator two weeks to produce the shipping documents. Who really 'owns' the cargo at any one time in this chain of twenty or more buyers and banks? Who 'owns' the cargo if one of the buyers or banks in the chain has gone bankrupt?

The short answer is – it is hard to say short of an expensive court hearing! It is certainly not something a master, who is merely carrying, not accounting for the trading of the cargo, can answer. It is not something which the person who believes he is the last buyer through a chain of valid buyers can answer either; he will be the most surprised if the chain has failed or by-passed him. Nor is it a solution to have these two least-informed people argue about it at the end of the dock when one is trying to turn his ship around and the other to take delivery of a very expensive cargo which was ordered for more reasons than just to pay demurrage.

Letters of indemnity

To date the industry solution has been to use letters of indemnity (LOI). These letters may be used in two ways: between the supposed last buyer who is demanding delivery of a cargo and the ship's master, and between any seller and his buyer. Essentially an LOI says that the issuer owns the goods and has the right to sell them or to take delivery if the documents are missing. Should the documents turn up the issuer will give them over to the buyer or master, but should another present them the issuer will hold the buyer or master safe from any claims in conversion or false sale. This letter does not take the place of a B/L, and in some ways it merely doubles the issuer's liability for missing or incorrect documents. They are used because most times most documents eventually turn up in the right place and in the meantime business can proceed.

But with oil cargoes costing tens of millions of dollars, demurrage charges and off-hire costs for tankers in the tens of thousands and potential lost sales through lost inventory, all extremely critical factors at a time when many oil traders, oil buyers, ship charterers and their banks are struggling to stay liquid, the question of who 'owns' the goods can no longer be treated as 'merely academic'. Having most documents appear in the right place most of the time leaves too much risk with which the LOI solution does not cope.

Substituting a waybill would be easier for the shipowners, but it does not suit the needs of buyers and their banks. New systems are valueless unless they first overcome the problem of transferability, and the pure electronic transfer of trade and transport documents is not possible under today's legal regime. What is left?

The SeaDocs system

Under the SeaDocs concept documents continue to be prepared

in their usual form and place. Then instead of trying to move them from master to seller, from seller to buyer, or his bank or their banks and back, and then to a new buyer and his bank etc, they would be taken to one or more central locations and kept there. All future trading, sighting of documents for such purposes as checking a letter of credit, arrangements for discharge of the cargo, etc, would take place through the medium of this central registry of documents. In this way SeaDocs is roughly modelled on the EUROCLEAR, CEDEL, SWIFT, TALISMAN and DTC systems for centrally clearing eurosecurities, money transfers and share certificates. By retaining the physical documents SeaDocs solves the critical problems faced by any electronic transfer system, that is uncertainty in law and questions as to the authenticity of the purported message.

Because the original documents survive there can be no greater doubt than exists today as to the intent of the parties or as to what law it is under. Users feel secure in using their own documents, procedures and operating systems. The useful features of a bill of lading are preserved, the document is only made to function better. The SeaDocs Registry Ltd is like a dedicated information interchange network between its participating members. In some ways SeaDocs could even reduce the uncertainty of the present system by making the information stored in trade documents more available than it is today to cargo buyers, if all the parties to a transaction so agree.

SeaDocs operates as an agent for its participant-members. It receives messages and then either sends out information as required or acts on a document in a prescribed manner. As agent for all interested parties the Registry can, for example, transfer the B/L on behalf of the seller as agent and receive it on behalf of the buyer as agent with electronic audit messages going to the affected participants. The Registry gets around the transfer problem by doing it internally; the problem of the letter of credit is more difficult.

SeaDocs and the banks: trade and transportation documents

Banks are said to need the physical documents in order to examine them on behalf of the buyer. What the bank is really saying is two things on behalf of the customer, and one on its own behalf:

The buyer wants the documents he agreed with the seller so that he knows the goods are of the right specification; and he needs the right pieces of paper with which to clear the goods.

The bank wants the title both as security and as a lever over the buyer.

This can still be accomplished with the insertion of SeaDocs although in a slightly different fashion from today. The Registry would continue to hold all documents but it would either make available an electronic true copy or certify to the banks that the documents have been checked and conform to the letter of credit/ sales agreement. The Registry could also create an electronic lien in favour of the bank who would have physically held the bill of lading. This 'lien' would work as follows. Although the buyer through a valid sales agreement would continue to be listed as the owner of the goods in the books of the Registry, the Registry would not instruct the captain to deliver until the bank (which would have held the physical B/L if it were available, pursuant to its financing agreement) agreed to allow the delivery of the cargo. Banks may have to change the wording of their letters of credit to include the words 'registered bill of lading' but this would be fine under the new UCP and can be done with a boiler plate agreement.

By preserving the mechanics of the transaction the Registry ensures that the position of the parties remains the same at law, but it speeds up the transaction by moving the information about faster and more reliably by electronic means. In a normal transaction it is the information in the paper which is the critical part. It is only in disputes that an authentic document (ie a piece of paper), is required. Under the Registry's rules the last holder of record always has the right to demand the documents back and can use them to take the other disputing party to court.

SeaDocs differentiated

Unlike DataFreight and CARDIS, SeaDocs is not computer, telecommunication or company specific; anyone with any secure mode of communication could access it from any port to any port for any carrier, buyer, seller or agent. To achieve this flexibility SeaDocs has to be inflexible in requiring all potential users to sign a binding agreement with the Registry.

SeaDocs system is also expensive to develop and run. The proposed fee structure looks minimal when set against the typical multi-million dollar value of a bulk cargo or even against the tens of thousands of dollars a ship can cost in demurrages if the master insists on his right to see the documents. It also looks very cost efficient for banks in terms of their checking role and desire to protect their security interests. However, it will be several years before economies of scale make it a competitive idea for general cargoes.

Critics of SeaDocs point out that it does not eliminate the paper, it only seeks to contain it. This is true in the case of SeaDocs Phase I. SeaDocs would actually work better in the hoped-for all electronic 'paperless cargo' environment.

Before moving into Phase II, however, more work must be done to create an environment for electronic 'paperless cargo' either by persuading courts and companies that valid checkable contracts can be made without being on paper and/or by demonstrating an authenticated solely electronic signature. A great deal of work is being done in this area by Messrs Hans Thompson and Knut Helge Reinskou and Professor Roger Henriksen.

Paperless cargo and electronic authenticity

These mainly Nordic initiatives have centred on using various cryptographic replacements for a signature.

Some of the ideas, for example the Public-Key Cryptography and Public Switch-Center Cryptography, require activities on the part of the message sender which may be seen to be akin to being 'signer-dependent'. Signer dependency is one of the three elements in authenticating a message. The other two are data dependent and interdependent. The easiest way to look at this is to consider why people want contracts in writing. If someone tries to change the writing on the paper it will show or if two parties dispute what they contracted about a third can see their intent and resolve the question; this is data dependency. If a person puts his signature to paper then one knows he had intent; this is signature dependency. The signature also presumes that the person read what is above his name – certainly a court will hold that he did; this is what is meant by interdependency.

SeaDocs Phase I overcomes the question of authenticity as follows: (a) the written document with signature is preserved; (b) all messages into the Registry must meet three tests – (i) each party's message must be confirmed by at least one or more other messages, (ii) messages are re-filed to the presumed sender and must be reacknowledged, and (iii) each message has a header code which is unique to sender and message as it must contain an element from the prior sender and from the computer acknowledgement message and (c) each participant signs a contract agreeing to this and authorising the Registry to act on its behalf in a specified manner. The Registry itself is insured against mistakes within its own system and for fraudulent acts on the part of its employees. Point (ii) is of course modelled on a bank money transfer test code which currently represents most authenticated messages.

INTERNATIONAL TRADE DATA INTERCHANGE SYSTEMS

Bernard Wheble

In a seminar directed to consideration of the 'Legal Implications of Electronic Banking', it is not unreasonable for speakers and participants to think basically of such problems in the simple context of electronic funds transfers, whether effected domestically or internationally. In turn, when concentrating on international electronic funds transfers, it is understandable if they are seen basically as clean, straightforward, inter-bank payment instructions, particularly having in mind the vast volume of such transfers which arise from inter-bank dealings in the foreign exchange markets of the world.

This may cause the fact to be overlooked that many international funds transfers stem from international trade transactions, and that this adds an extra dimension to the problem, it becoming necessary to consider more than questions raised by speeding the funds transfers by electronic means. The question of what may, perhaps, be referred to as 'goods transfers', has also to be considered. In respect of international trade, before there can be an entitlement to a funds transfer – especially when a documentary letter of credit is involved – there is need for a reverse direction transfer of trade data and, in many cases as a more complicating factor, a transfer of rights in the goods in respect of which the funds transfer is to be made.

Trade data interchange

Traditionally this type of trade data and rights in goods transfer has been effected by means of 'paper', traditional documents such as the commercial invoice, a regulatory document such as the certificate of origin, an insurance document such as a shipper's declaration under an open cover and a document of title to the goods in transit, such as a negotiable bill of lading for sea transport or a negotiable combined transport document, however called, for multi-modal transport of unitised cargo (often in the 'big boxes' called 'containers'), possession of such transport document enabling the holder to claim the goods at destination.

But 'paper' can – and all too often does – cause hold-ups, as it tends to move from exporting to importing country more slowly than the goods themselves; and hold-up of cargo at destination delays its entry into the commerce of the buyer, renders the goods open to extra risks of loss and/ or damage 'on quay' and may give rise to expensive demurrage costs.

Therefore a system of electronic international trade data interchange becomes highly desirable, a trade 'near equivalent' to the banking electronic funds transfer system.

SeaDocs type of solution

Earlier speakers have given clues as to possibilities for this development. Dr Arora, speaking of the 'truncation' of cheques, has suggested that:

> 'The truncation process could be extended to other instruments which have previously to be presented physically.'

Professor Ellinger, speaking in the context of the replacement of bills of exchange by an electronic funds transfer system, has carried this idea a stage further, in his comment that:

> 'It is possible to think in terms of a centre in which such documents are recorded and stored and which handles all the operations required in respect of them.'

The development of a system of truncation and the establishment of such a centre in the context of the international use of the traditional document of title to goods in transit, has been shown to be a possibility – and a probable not too distant reality – by the report of the Chase Manhattan Bank 'SeaDocs' project. This plans to do just what Dr Arora and Professor Ellinger have suggested. It will provide an international 'electronic transfer of title to goods in transit system', even though the system will be based upon the continued existing use of the traditional paper document.

Non-negotiable documents solution

The SeaDocs innovative thinking has thus much to commend it, at any rate where bulk cargoes traded in during course of transit are concerned. It does, however, cling to the tradition of a 'paper' document – and a negotiable one at that – with the consequent restraints imposed by the requirement of endorsement and delivery. In fact, reduced to basics, the SeaDocs concept is simply an ingenious technique for meeting these requirements, whilst at the same time avoiding the restraints inherent in them.

This does, however, provoke thought as to the need for a document of carriage to continue to possess the characteristic of 'negotiability'. True, an early amending protocol to the Warsaw Convention on Carriage by Air does sanction the issue of a negotiable airway bill. But, commercially, such a document does not make sense: no-one would be willing to pay – and at a higher freight rate – for his goods to travel quickly, and then sit at destination waiting for the arrival of the negotiable document to set them free to move again.

The development in transport technology during the past two decades (the unitized handling of cargo in containers and the natural sequel of a 'door-to-door' movement of the container on one contract of multi-modal carriage) has so speeded the movement of the goods as, to a large extent, to make nonsense of the use of the negotiable document in other modes of transport also.

Consequently, the non-negotiable waybill has been developed – and is gradually being introduced into use – for goods moving by sea or on a multi-modal contract of carriage.

Trade data interchange systems (TDIS)

This suggests the next development – which will lead to an entirely new 'ball game' and which could be closely linked with developments in electronic funds transfer systems – ie a replacement of the paper document by electronic interchange of the data.

Speaking of the bill of exchange, Professor Ellinger has expressed the view that:

'There can be no doubt that if the problem of "signing" were solved it would be equally possible to transfer or deliver an electronically created bill by means of a teletransmission.'

So far as trade data interchange is concerned the position is, perhaps, easier. The 'symbolic' function problem associated with a paper document can be met by the agreed acceptance of non-negotiability, as in the case of the waybill. The 'informative' function can be equally well met by data stored in, and retrievable from, a computer memory bank and transmitted electronically between computers. The 'evidential' function can be met by means of authentication other than 'signature' – banks are long accustomed to 'authenticate' cables and telexes by types of test-keys, some of which can also verify the data content of the message. The SWIFT system is an outstanding example of this in inter-bank electronic communications.

Legal problems

Where problems are more likely to arise is in the legal field; uncertainty as to the position in law with electronic data interchange, because the existing law has been 'paper based', ie incorporates the concept of something in writing, such as the Bills of Exchange Act requirement of 'an unconditional order in writing'. As pointed out in a Scandinavian study (Nordipro Special Paper Number 2 – Legal Questions of Trade Facilitation):

'It is important to understand the essential difference from the legal angle between a document and automatic data transfer. The ordinary export document retains its identity: a signature on that document will remain there, whether made by an authorised person or not – and even if it is forged. Corrections and additions will also show on the document itself. Automated data transfer, on the other hand, by its very nature, has a completely different characteristic. Once fed into the computer the data seem to lose their identity; they are retained in a computer memory and become accessible only by computer programs. Here also there is a legal aspect – the problem of regulatory law. Paper-borne data is acceptable – but with a known specified legal format, data content and method of authentication. A corresponding legal acceptability for data produced automatically or electronically may not exist.'

Further, what specific law does exist may not necessarily address the point which is commercially important. Fraud with paper documents has, unfortunately, become a major problem in recent years, with a false data input on the document. This may, perhaps, be even more a potential hazard with data produced, transmitted and stored electronically. Yet as Martin Karmel points out:

'S.5 of the Civil Evidence Act 1968 has been described as one of turgid complexity, elaborately concerned to exclude evidence tainted by technical malfunction while making no effort to ensure the reliability of input.'

INTERNATIONAL TRADE DATA INTERCHANGE SYSTEMS

This relates to one area of 'security' and 'security' in the widest sense is essential in any interchange of money and goods. There is also, however, the more legal aspect, the right of access and/or the prevention of access to stored data, for example, and the right to amend it, or to add to or subtract from the stored data. The existing law based on paper-borne data does not necessarily give the legal control which would remove fear of fault, change or fraud in input, storage and transmission of data.

Nor can it be automatically assumed that evidentiary requirements will be legally satisfied. In its recommendation number 14 the Economic Commission for Europe Working Party on International Trade Facilitation states that:

> 'signatures are used to identify and confirm data. They are readily accepted as proof in Courts of Law.'

But that same recommendation also recognises that insistence on a signature is often the result of the non-thinking inertia of 'we always have signed documents, so we always must'. This attitude of mind is perhaps well illustrated by the story, possibly apocryphal, that:

> 'one day a "classified" document arrived on the desk of the man whose job was to sort documents and memoranda in a big governmental department. Although he had never received such an important document before, he read it, decided who should receive it and sent it on. Next day it came back to him with a note saying "you were not supposed to read this. Erase your initials – and initial your erasure".'

On the other hand, there may be a mandatory legal requirement of 'signature' – possibly limited to a manual signature, and as the Economic Commission for Europe recommendation 14 also points out:

> 'where a formal obligation of signature exists, a name will continue to be required until the obligation is abolished'.

Nevertheless, it also goes on to stress that:

> 'a valid replacement for signature can be offered by computer systems, giving verifiable guarantees as to the identity of the parties; these could permit themselves to recognise messages exchanged by a system and to sign a written agreement to this effect'.

Filling the legal vacuum

This contractual approach to the problem of a legal vacuum would appear to be favoured by Professor Goode, since he has pointed out that:

> 'there is much to be said for taking the initiative in formulating clear and acceptable rules which fairly balance these legitimate requirements of the parties in an electronic age, the rules being incorporated by express reference in written contracts in the same way as the Uniform Customs and Practice for Documentary Credits'.

This is a particularly interesting 'forward look', since the formulation of rules of this nature has been a major task of the Scandinavian group during 1984 and, in fact, its draft rules have now gone forward to the International Chamber of Commerce (hopefully for consideration by a wider based *ad hoc* group), it being felt that the International Chamber of Commerce is the best platform for their launching.

These rules are for 'communication agreements' and:
(a) are directed at users of a TDIS – whether the DEDIST of Scandinavia, the CARDIS of the USA or any other agreed system;
(b) apply only by voluntary and explicit acceptance by such TDIS users;
(c) define the terms used in the rules;
(d) deal with questions of security, verification and confirmation of messages, authentication of the communicating parties, privacy, storage of data and liability.

Conclusion

This will not, of course, be a final solution: nor can it be a full one. For security reasons it could be useful to require the encryption of messages – but the national data law of some countries forbids the transborder transmission of encrypted messages.

This indicates another area where solutions will have to be found. Without so intending, some national data laws, by their drafting, restrict the transborder flow by electronics of trade data which must pass between selling and buying countries for the purposes of completing the transaction – and which still can, and do, pass freely if 'paper-borne'.

INTERNATIONAL TRADE DATA INTERCHANGE SYSTEMS

Trade data interchange may seem an area somewhat remote from electronic funds transfers – but it is an essential part of the concept of electronic banking. No-one would dissociate funds transfers from documentary credits, anymore than they would ignore the trade data transfer by means of paper documents. But, in time, electronic communication possibilities may well lead to the 'documentless documentary credit' – to 'funds transfer' instructions being held in abeyance in a data bank at the instance of the buyer until specified 'goods transfer' instructions are fed in at the instance of the seller, completing the connection and releasing the funds to the seller and the goods to the buyer.

Index

AGENCY
  agent,
    commitment to pay by, when irrevocable, 19
    payment, authority to accept, 22
    unauthorised instructions to bank to pay by, 70
  EFT, agency relationships in, vii, 35

ASSIGNMENT
  assignee, right of, to demand payment, 30
  EFT distinguished from, 35

AVIATION
  airway bill, 114, 125

BACS
  batching, period of, vi, 24
  credit transfer through, when irrevocable, 22
  deferred payment, problems of, 38
  functions, 8, 31
  history, 8
  operating times, 8
  payment instructions irrevocable, when, 21
  'sponsored customers', 8, 31

BANK
  bankers' books, definition of, 46
  Bankers' Books Evidence Act, 1879, 2, 45
  cash card-holder, liability where breach by, 90
  collecting, liability of,
    CHAPS transaction, where, 76
    cheques, for, 73
  commitment to pay, 17
  communication lines, interception of messages along, 60
  confidentiality of customers' data, 64
  contract with customer, specific, viii, 2
  customer relationship with, viii, 2, 83
  duty to exercise reasonable skill and care, 75
  employees, liability for acts of, 76
  forged cheques or payment instructions, 70, 71
  fraud by employees, 60
  identification of authorised persons, contract term for, 93
  indemnity to,
    cheques mechanically signed or completed, where, 84, 89
    direct debiting system, under, 85, 90

INDEX

    independent contractors, liability for, 77
    insolvency of, where commitment to pay, 17
    instructions by customer,
        ambiguous instructions, 68
        company directors, unauthorised acts of, 70
        enforceable liability of customer, debit to discharge, 70
        forged signature of customer, 70, 71
        fraud or misrepresentation, transaction vitiated by, 69
        mistake, transaction invalidated by, 69
        unauthorised signature by or for customer, 70
    inter-bank agreements as to commitment and payment, 26
    liability of,
        breakdown in system or computer, 63
            restriction on liability for, 63, 97
        direct debit instruction, 90
        errors, for, of originating bank, 63
        exemption or restriction of, viii, 63, 88, 93, 96
        supervening events, effect of, 92
        telephone instruction, where, 90
        telex or telegraphic instruction, 90
        unauthorised payment instruction, as to, viii, 70
        vicarious, 76
    'lien' in favour of, by SeaDocs Registry, 120
    mistake in cheque, liability for, 89
    paying, liability of,
        CHAPS transaction, where, 75
        cheques, for, 73
        recovery and restitution, right of, 76
    SeaDocs system, use of, by, 119
    security systems, duty to operate, viii, 60, 64, 77
    software and hardware, representations as to use of, 93
    standing order to, 35
    statement, whether duty to check, ix, 62
    telephone, instructions by, 84, 85, 90
    telex or telegraph, instructions by, 84, 90
    third parties, liability for acts of, 77
    transfer, grounds for refusal to make, 64

BANK GIRO
    credit vouchers, transfer of, 6

BANKING
    development of automated systems, 57
    diagram of transfer of funds, 16
    off-line electronic systems, 8
    on-line electronic systems, vi, 9
    paper-based systems, v, 5, 57

INDEX

BANKRUPTCY
    foreign correspondent, of, where deferred payment, 37

BILL OF EXCHANGE. *See also* NEGOTIABLE INSTRUMENTS
    acceptance credits, 40
    c.i.f. document, accompanying, 40
    commitment to pay irrevocable, when, 20
    deferred payment EFT, creation by, 41
    discounting of, 40
    dishonour of, 43
    documentary credits, 40
    forged, rights of recovery where, 80
    nature of, 2, 41
    presentment, 43
    property, as, 2, 42
    recovery, right of, and prompt notice of claim, 80
    string of contracts, as, 2, 41
    transferable, must be, 42
    transmission of, electronic, 38

BILL OF LADING
    CARDIS system, 116
    conversion, tort of, 112
    history of, 112
    importance of, 112
    oil cargoes, use for, 117
    SeaDocs system, x, 118

CASH OR CREDIT CARD
    card-holder, obligations on, 90, 96
    EFTPOS transaction, use in, 11
    erroneous debiting of account, burden of proof of, 50
    loss or misuse,
        liability of card-holder, limit on, 52, 61, 90, 96
        notification of, liability after, 61, 90, 95, 96
    PIN,
        burden of proof as to non-disclosure, 50
        duty not to disclose, 85, 90, 93
    unathorised withdrawal of funds by, 84, 90

CHAPS
    batching, 24
    commercial and non-settlement bank customers, rights and liabilities of, 67, 81
    commitment to pay, 23
    customer and bank, relationship of, 75, 85, 91
    defensive devices to prevent unauthorised operation of system, 77

133

INDEX

    duty on bank to exercise reasonable skill and care, 75
    financial limits on transactions, 10
    function of, 9, 31, 74
    gateways, 10, 31
    guaranteed payments, 10, 79
    malfunction in system, 84, 85, 91
    mistake, recovery by paying bank where, 80
    operating times, 10, 32
    ordinary customer of settlement bank, rights and liabilities of, 67
    payment, instruction for, through,
        collecting bank, liability of, 76
        commercial customer, direct instructions by, to CHAPS, 81
        forged signature of customer, 70
        form of, 67
        improper instructions, liability for, where direct connection, 82
        irrevocable, when, 23
        paying bank, obligations of, 72, 75
        revocation of, 78
        unauthorised signature by or for customer, 70
    payment message,
        acknowledgement of, 78
        cancellation or abandonment of, 78
    recovery, rights of, 79
    revocation instruction, 78
    same day settlement, 9, 31
        paying bank, liability of, 23, 68, 92
    security systems, duty of care as to, viii, 77
    settlement bank, duty of, to customer, 68
    transfer of payment, 32
    void or voidable transaction, rights of recovery where, 79

CHEQUES
    clearing. *See* CLEARING
    collection bank, liability of, 73
    commitment to pay irrevocable, when, 20
    dishonoured, 107
    indorsed, 110
    mechanically signed or printed, 84, 89
        indemnity to bank, 84, 89
    mistake or malfunction, effect of, 84, 89
    paying bank
        duty to act within mandate, 74
        liability of, 73
    return of incorrect, 106
    signature,
        forged, 70, 71
        verification of ix, 3, 110

truncation,
  advantages of, 108, 109
  forgery or fraud, problems of, 110
  international developments, ix, 109
  partial or full, 3, 108
  problems of, ix, 3, 110
  process, stages of, ix, 108

CLEARING
  Bankers' Automated Clearing Services (BACS). *See* BACS
  cheque, truncation, 5, 107
  Credit, 6, 8, 107
  General, 5, 7, 105, 106
  inter-branch system, 7
  Irish cheques, 7
  Scottish cheques, 7
  settlement, daily and final, 6, 106
  statistics, 7
  Town, 6, 8, 105
  types of system, 105
  'walks' system, 7

COMPANY
  unauthorised instructions to bank by directors, 70

COMPUTER
  bankers' books produced by, 46
  breakdown, liability of bank for, 63
  definition of, 56
  fraud where access to system, 59
  statements produced by, admissibility of, vii, 46
    certificate by person responsible for operating computer, 54
    civil proceedings, 48, 54
    criminal proceedings, 47
    notice relating to statement produced by computer, 54
    Order 38, Rule 24, 54
    presumption that instrument in working order, 48

CONTRACT
  arbitration, agreement to submit to, 103
  equality of bargaining power, 85
  exclusion clauses,
    commercial contracts, 87
    consumer contracts, 87, 102
    electronic fund transfer, where, by bank, 63, 88, 96
    negligence, liability for, 101
    reasonableness test, 88, 102

INDEX

    'guidelines' for applying, 103
    standard term contracts, 87, 88, 102
    Unfair Contract Terms Act, 88, 101–104
frustration, 92
implied terms, 88
supervening events, effect of, 92
unconscionable bargains set aside, 86
Unfair Contract Terms Act 1977, 87, 101–104

CONVERSION
    bill of lading, delivery of, to wrong party, 112

CREDIT CARD. *See* CASH OR CREDIT CARD

CREDIT TRANSFER
    payment instruction irrevocable, when, 21
    system, functions of, 107

CURRENCY
    forward exchange contract, 38

DEFERRED PAYMENT
    forward exchange contract, 38
    undertaking,
        EFT, use of, 29, 33, 38
        paper-based, 29

DIRECT DEBIT
    bank, liability of, for unauthorised debit, 91
    commitment to pay irrevocable, when 21
    indemnity to bank where wrongly debited, 85, 90
    malfunction in arrangements, 84, 85, 91

EFT
    assignment, not an, 35
    automatic clearing house (ACH), use of, 24
    batching, vi, 24
    commitment to pay, 23
    customer, advantages for, ix
    defects in hardware or software, 2, 62
    deferred payment undertakings by, 29, 33, 38
    definition of,
        UNCITRAL, by, 58
        United States legislation, in, 45, 95
    delivery of message, time for, vi
    error resolution,
        damages where breach by financial institution, 96, 99

'error', meaning of, 99
United States legislation, 95, 98
errors arising in relation to, 62
exclusion clauses in bank's terms of business, viii, 63, 93, 96
frustration of contract, 92
growth of, 1, 57
instruction to bank to pay, as, 35
legal implications of, 1
malfunction of sytem or computer,
   bank, restriction on liability of, 63, 93, 97
   liability for, 25, 63
negotiable instrument, not a, 34
payment complete, time when, 25
stop a pre-authorised transfer, procedure to, 95
supervening events, effect of, 92
unauthorised transfers, customers' liability for, 51, 96, 100
   burden of proof, 101
   limit of liability, 51, 61, 96, 100
   notification by customer, 96, 100
   PIN, burden of proof as to disclosure of, 2, 50
UNCITRAL draft legal guide on, 62
unitised transfers, 24

EFTPOS
credit or debit card, use of, 11
features of system, 10, 94
Personal Identification Number (PIN), use of, 11
retail payment transaction, steps in, 11, 94

ESTOPPEL
forged signature of customer, as to, 71

EVIDENCE
bankers' books, definition of, 46
Bankers' Books Evidence Act 1879, 2, 45
business records, 48
computer, admissibility of documents produced by, vii, 46
   certificate by person responsible for operating computer, 54
   civil proceedings, 48, 53
   criminal proceedings, 47
   notice relating to statements produced by computer, 54
   Order 38, Rule 24, 54
microfilm records, admissibility of, 46
Police and Criminal Evidence Act 1984, 47
presumption that mechanical instruments in working order, 48
proof of ATM transactions, problems of, vii, 50
trade data interchange systems (TDIS), problems in, 126, 127
unauthorised debit, burden of proof as to, 2, 50

INDEX

FORGERY
  bill of exchange, of, rights of recovery where, 80
  carelessness by customer, 72
  CHAPS transaction, in, rights of recovery where, 79
  forged signature of customer
    cheque, on, 70, 71
    instruction to bank, on, 70
    ratification of, 71

FRAUD
  bank employees, by, 60
  bank, instructions to, where transactions vitiated by, 69
  communication lines, interception of EFT messages along, 60
  computer system, access to, viii, 59
  corporate customers, where terminal links with, 60
  customer, duty of care of, to prevent, 61
  definition, in relation to EFT, 59
  employee, by, 59
  passwords for corporate customers, 61
  rescission for, 69

INDEMNITY
  bank, to,
    cheques mechanically printed, where, 84, 89
    direct debiting system, under, 85, 90
  Letters of Indemnity (LOI), 118

INSOLVENCY
  bank, of, where commitment to pay, 17
  bankruptcy of foreign correspondent, 37

INTERNATIONAL CHAMBER OF COMMERCE
  rules for communication agreements, 128

INTERNATIONAL TRADE
  trade data interchange, x, 123
    SeaDocs concept for, 124
  trade data interchange systems (TDIS), 125
    evidence, requirements of, 126, 127
    fraud and security, 126
    ICC rules, 128
    legal problems, 126
    signature, need for, 127

IRELAND
  cheques, clearing, 7

INDEX

LIMITATIONS OF ACTIONS
payment vitiated by mistake or fraud, recovery of, 81

MERCANTILE LAW
history of, 112

MISREPRESENTATION
bank, instructions to, where transaction vitiated by, 69

MISTAKE
bank, instructions to, where transaction vitiated by, 69
CHAPS payment, in, recovery by paying bank where, 80
cheque, in mechanically produced, liability for, 84, 89
derivative transaction, effect on, of, 69
limitation period where payment vitiated by, 81

NEGLIGENCE
breakdown of system or computer, liability for, 63
contributory, by customer, 61
exclusion or restriction of liability, 88, 101

NEGOTIABLE INSTRUMENTS
bill of exchange. *See* BILL OF EXCHANGE
deferred payment EFT, and, 39
EFT distinguished from, 34
replacement by records in EFT network, 29, 43
transmission of, electronic, 38

OIL
cargoes, problems of ownership of, 117
commodity traders, needs of, 116

PAYMENT
agent, authority of, to accept, 22
authority to pay distinguished from obligation to pay, 30
cheque, obligation where, 30
commitment to pay,
  agent, by, 19
  BACS, direct debit through, 21
  bank, by, 17
  cheque or bill, where, 20
  credit transfer, where, 21
  direct debit, paper-based, 21
  EFT methods, 23
complete, time when, vi, 22
  EFT methods, automated, 25
  tangible payment, methods, 22

INDEX

    credit transfer, diagram showing, 16
    debit collection, diagram showing, 16
    deferred. *See* DEFERRED PAYMENT
    instruction, when irrevocable, vi, 19
    inter-bank agreements as to, 26
    meaning of, 16
    messages,
        electronic media, by, vi
        magnetic material, on, v
        paper-based, v
    refusal to accept, 25
    settlement, distinguished from, 18
    undertaking to pay, distinguished from, 17

PERSONAL IDENTIFICATION NUMBER (PIN)
    card-holder, limit on liability of, for misuse, 52, 61, 90
    customers, duty of care on, 90, 96
    EFTPOS system, use in, 11
    non-disclosure of,
        burden of proof as to, 50
        duty on card-holder, 85, 90, 93

PROMISSORY NOTE
    transmission of, electronic, 39

SCOTLAND
    cheques, clearing, 7

SETTLEMENT
    Credit Clearing, 6
    General Clearing, 5, 6
    meaning of, 18
    payment, distinguished from, 18
    Town Clearing, 6

SHIPPING DOCUMENTS
    authentication of, 121
    bill of lading. *See* BILL OF LADING
    Cargo Data Interchange System (CARDIS), 115
    cryptographic replacements for signatures, 121
    DataFreight system, 114–115, 116
    history of, 112
    importance of, 111
    Letters of Indemnity (LOI), 118
    oil cargoes, for, 116, 117

SeaDocs system, x, 116, 118
  advantages, 119
  authenticity, checks on, 121
  bank, relationship with, 119
  flexibility and cost, 120
  'lien' in favour of bank, 120
  paperless cargo, developments for, 121
  Registry, work of, x, 119
  trade data interchange, for international, 124
signature, importance of, 113
standardisation, problems of, 115
waybills, 114–116

SIGNATURE
  cheque, on,
    forged, 70, 71
    verification of, ix, 3, 110
  payment instruction, on, forged, 70, 71
  transport and shipping documents, on, 113

SWIFT
  function of, 12, 32
  history of, 12
  transmission of messages, 13, 33
  'value date' and time of payment, 37

TRANSPORT
  documents,
    Cargo Data Interchange System (CARDIS), 115
    container cargoes, computerised waybills for, 114
    DataFreight system, 114–115, 116
    SeaDocs system. *See* SHIPPING DOCUMENTS
    signature, importance of, 113
    waybills, 114
  industry, problems of, 111
  multimodal, documents for, 123, 125
  oil cargoes, 116, 117
  ownership of cargo, problems of, 117

UNCITRAL
  electronic funds transfer,
    definition of, 58
    draft legal guide on, 62
  fraud in relation to EFT, definition of, 59

UNITED STATES
  bank,
    exemptions from liability, 64

INDEX

    refusal to make a transfer, grounds for, 64
    statements, whether duty to inspect, 63
    transfer of funds, reversibility of, 25
    cheque truncation, 110
    Electronic Funds Transfer Act, 1978
        credit card or PIN, liability of card-holder for misuse of, 51, 61, 95, 96
        definition of EFT, 45, 95
        errors, investigation and correction of, 95, 98
        provisions, 98–101
        stop a pre-authorised transfer, procedure to, 95
        unauthorised transfers, customer's liability for, 61, 96, 100

WAYBILL
    airway bill, 114, 125
    Atlantic Container Lines (ACL) system, 114
    Cargo Key Receipt, 114
    container cargoes, computerised for, 114
    DataFreight system, 114–115, 116
    non-negotiable, use of, 125